SYSTEM OF NOVELTIES

 PARK BOOKS

Dawn Finley and Mark Wamble
Interloop—Architecture

Table of Contents

8	Part 1	Information—Shape
		9° House
		Symonds (+) Teaching Laboratories
		Open Transfer
		Notes No. 1
84	Part 2	Procedure—Assembly
		48' House
		Klip
		E-X-I-T
		Tending,(blue)
		Notes No. 2
162	Part 3	Material—Detail
		Yoga Studio and Garden
		Hempstead Research Center
		J-Camp
		Inside Corner
		Notes No. 3
268		Credits

System of Novelties
Interloop—Architecture

In 1972 Charles and Ray Eames produced *SX-70* for the Polaroid Corporation. Part advertisement, part sales tool, and part instructional guide, this eleven-minute film introduced Edwin Land's revolutionary SX-70 instant reflex camera using arresting, technically innovative visual sequences. Composites of film clips, detailed still photographs, drawing notation overlays, and sound are used to track, step by step, the camera's material, procedural, and informational components, as well as its intricate mechanics of ephemerality. The user selects a human activity and directs the camera toward it. Light passes through the lens and reflects off tiny mirrors within the body that houses the camera's precisely assembled components. A single sheet of composite film is exposed and quickly developed via the delicate, coordinated, mechanical movements of disparate parts. A voice-over by the American physicist Philip Morrison then describes the camera as an invention that links materials, technologies, processes, research, and artisanry with people's diverse needs. "No single thread wove this invention; not lens, not moving mirror, not film chemistry, not clever circuits. They are coordinate parts of a single strategy working together . . . this is a system. Call it a system of novelties."

Morrison's phrase, "system of novelties," positions a seemingly simple object—in this case, a novel instant camera—as resulting from specialized expertise, materials, and manufacturing that have been coordinated and synthetically combined through design. *System of novelties* thus asks us to consider each designed artifact not as a discrete work but as a coordinated *instance*, one design manifestation or registration among the infinite combinatorial possibilities of the potential and contingent. The camera, in this view, can no longer be understood in isolation from the operative, technological, or even cultural conditions that brought it into being.

The SX-70, the Eames film proposes, cannot be extricated from the larger network of material, technological, and electronic systems that allowed it to emerge through design and assembly. The camera is finally engaged through human activity in space and time, becoming an active participant in the dynamic social systems of the world. The SX-70 represents a scalable set of relationships, coordinated in a novel way in a cultural artifact whose significance is dependent on both its means of production and its subsequent interactions in the world.

Architecture, too, is a part of the world and therefore dependent upon a range of complex formal and operational systems. Systems are the media through which architecture participates in, influences, and transforms the world. Acknowledging and productively engaging systems through design requires nimble, diverse modes of contemporary thinking and making. In short, architecture is a vital participant in the ongoing dynamic formation of the world.

The term *novelty* is often assumed to imply "new for the sake of new." In design, *novelty* most often refers to the modest or superficial refinement of an already existing article or construction. Novelty can be individual and subjective or shared and collective (e.g., among those who share a common culture and traditions). Yet from a legal and procedural perspective—for example,

Introduction

that of the U.S. Patent and Trademark Office—novelty describes specific forms, conditions, or details that have not previously been disclosed publicly, including nonvisual, technical aspects of architectural work. The U.S. Patent and Trademark Office categorically defines these conditions of novelty as "design" or "utility." We consider these various definitions as collectively forming a more complex picture of novelty as a disciplinary asset (an ambition) that is arrived at through aesthetic, technical, and performative conditions. The term *system* is a useful complement to *novelty*, expanding the scope of the latter's commonplace connotation to encompass a more nuanced set (i.e., a network) of understandings, methods, and outcomes.

As a descriptor for our work, *system of novelties* is benevolently expansive. We regard our practice and all of our productions as a system of novelties, and we consider each individual project a system of novelties. The elasticity and scalability of the term are useful and instructive. At the macro level, our design work is a collection of idiosyncratic projects that range in scale, type, and complexity—from institutional campus strategies, cultural institutions, and historic building additions to single-family houses, architectural hardware, and emergency life-safety fixtures—each project informed by a nonlinear (nonhierarchical) reflective sequence of work that precedes it. However, scale, type, and complexity are not what connect our projects. Rather, they share systems of research: informational, procedural, and material. Examined at the micro level, each project reveals a unique set of circumstances, constraints, and constituents. Disparate, contingent, and congruent systems are sorted and synthesized in each design proposal.

Of particular value for our practice are the novel mediations—between physical and operational systems—that yield consequences for architecture and architectural practice. That is, the pairing of systems and novelty creates the conditions for architectural knowledge production. We cultivate research and initiate open-ended explorations with deliberate determination and cautious optimism. The results, or effects, are not always visible but often implicate those processes that precede and follow an architectural project. We thus engage each project for its specificities and exigencies, always assessing the way we work as much as the work itself.

The aim of the present volume is to explicate the elasticity of the system concept by describing the trajectory of our practice over two decades. Three pairs of research topics—Information/Shape, Procedure/Assembly, Material/Detail—frame eleven representative projects. The topics provide provisional lenses for positioning the works (i.e., identifying their biases) and broadly connect design issues across scale, duration, type, and medium to demonstrate the persistent inclusiveness of our methods. The pairing of terms is significant. Individually, each one has a clear meaning in architecture; paired, each constituent term collectively augments and biases the other. While the projects are presented as distinct entities through comprehensive drawings, diagrams, images, photographs, and texts, the collective format resists the discrete, siloing effect of the monograph typology.

Critical to each of the eleven projects is the knowledge, techniques, and references that accumulated over time with other projects. To address this more inclusive view of architectural projects and practice, each of the three parts is supplemented with expanded graphic footnotes that trace connections among the unique, complex systems deployed in design. Often an inefficient process, design requires time and space to incubate and flourish—to lead us to the next possibility.

The book's format is intended to present and explicate a model of practice rather than rehearse a collection of discrete, seemingly effortless projects— the coin of most architectural monographs of this type. What they hide—what we wish to reveal—is the complex, often messy research directives with which most contemporary architecture offices must contend. While such an approach is not necessarily new, formulating and communicating new modes in the field's evolving, collective practice substantiates a unique system of novelties. The graphic structure employed in the present volume delicately assembles a diverse array of architectural paths, some productive, others unavailing, and many in-between.

Part 1

Information—
Shape

Interloop—Architecture

Information—
Shape

16   9° House

38   Symonds (+)
Teaching Laboratories

52   Open Transfer

72   Notes No. 1

Information comes in abundance and in many forms. For architects, information can be defined as the disparate objects, operations, facts, and attributes that surround and potentially shape a given design problem. In contemporary practice, architects must with each project determine anew what constitutes vital information and develop flexible, pragmatic means to select, edit, and creatively sort the diverse and often complex sets of data that must be accounted for.

In our office, to address this complexity, we often first develop and deploy a clear organizational and graphic armature, or *shape*, for each project. Shape is a geometric, two- or three-dimensional outline (boundary) that provides limited but specific organizational constraints. In architecture, that outline most commonly takes form through a diagram or simplified drawing. Shape is abstract yet legible, scalable, and elastic. It provides a comprehensible framework that serves as a reference when addressing the necessary demands of architecture. (While somewhat comparable, our use of the term should not be confused with contemporary discourse that values shape as an easy, arbitrary, graphic operation.) For us, shape is deliberate and precise, while also graphic. Our use of shape is not limited to the design of any one specific architectural element but applies to a diverse range of such, including building enclosures, built-in furniture, and open-air structures.

We strategically pair *shape* with *information* to foreground what we believe to be the fundamental conditions of architecture. The former, a calibrated disciplinary tool, asserts spatial boundaries upon the latter, thus rendering malleable the complex influences that each architectural project engenders.

In our work, shape is initiated first in plan as a simplified line drawing, or diagram, that includes no extraneous information beyond the organizational concept. The diagram, or diagram set, serves as a recurring reference throughout the design process, providing both guidance and resistance to the project's development. These diagrams are undoubtedly spatial and organizational, yet they offer no clues about the material, structural, or assembly aspects of architecture. Their geometric clarity and simplified representation (a line drawing) deny material specificity, performance, and characteristics.

Our interest is not to build or execute the diagram as an architectural demonstration; in fact, we actively resist such. We privilege the graphic and organizational legibility of shape in order to challenge the (material, structural, programmatic, technological, historical) complexity of architecture's environment. The graphic clarity of the diagram is retained as the project develops. Our approach to the architecture's elaboration is equally deliberate, although distinct in ambition. This superimposition of shape and information allows their unique specificities to coexist, often in tension. Shape demands simplicity, while information burdens complexity. Our work attempts to keep these two conditions legible and comprehensible.

Three projects that examine the distinct, varied roles of shape and information in architecture are 9° House (a historic residential addition), Symonds (+) Teaching Laboratories (a set of experimental technology classrooms), and Open Transfer (a transportation infrastructure). These projects each more narrowly define *information* as the programmatic, material, structural, technological, or historical aspects of an architectural work. The first and third take existing architectural types in new directions by overlaying culturally charged material selections that elicit unexpected domestic and urban experiences. The second project balances the intangible aspects of digital technologies with the physical componentry of architecture.

9° House

The 9° House challenges the complex, often didactic, visual and representational concerns when designing additions for historic buildings. The design consciously (and conceptually) sidesteps the conventions of contrast (claims of differentiation) or reverence (simulation of the given artifact) that are often conflated with historical architectural additions by producing a synthetic hybrid using geometric distinction.

In 1955, when the original house was developed by architects Wilson, Morris, Crain and Anderson, who later designed the Astrodome, modernism was just beginning to infiltrate architectural design and planning in Houston. The Menil House by Philip Johnson was completed in 1948, while Mies van der Rohe's first addition for the Museum of Fine Arts, Houston was completed ten years later. Conflicted by modernist ambitions in massing and brick detailing at its base, the original two-story house overlaid more traditional residential standards of clapboard siding and a pitched roof. The tension visible on the exterior continued within the interior. For example, the rational open floor plan of the main living space was finished with elaborate crown molding and ornate wood paneling. Our design for the addition acknowledged these initial incongruities, treating them as both a caution and an inspiration.

We first developed the design in plan, simplifying the organizational concept through two-dimensional diagrams. In 9° House, the base geometry of the addition skews nine degrees to fill the vacant southwest corner of the property. Every detail of the addition conforms to this nine-degree shift, making the interior transition between the old and new architecture organizationally explicit through a striking optical effect.

While interior material finishes and exterior rainscreen cladding serve to unify the new and old, the orthogonal geometry of the 1955 house is continued in one axis of the addition but shifts nine degrees in plan in the other axis, resulting in a sequence of parallelogram spaces and built-in elements that experientially mark the transition from old to new. The angular geometry is not a plan motif repeated indifferently; rather, it is a highly structured spatial device that foregrounds the durational performance of the house rather than its appearance.

The material continuity of the interior (terrazzo flooring, bright white walls and ceilings) is punctuated by idiosyncratic, custom built-in furniture pieces (bench, credenza, counter) and architectural elements (stairs, guardrail, and column) that are strategically distributed throughout the shared public areas of the 9° House. These object-like pieces and elements provide notable material and color distinction (large-veined marble, polished stainless steel, vibrant yellow paint, finished hardwood, leather upholstery), drawing the eye toward the spaces of domestic activity they define and support. The overlay of these furniture-scale elements provides a secondary organization to the house that both conforms to the geometric logic of the nine-degree shift—the bench cushion is a parallelogram in plan—and resists the distinction between old and new portions of the house by providing an even field of objects to unify the two.

<u>Symonds (+)
Teaching
Laboratories</u>

One of our earliest projects in the 1990s, Symonds Teaching Laboratory, navigates the introduction and integration of digital tools and technologies to university research and teaching environments. This was a critical moment in our design thinking that explicitly shifted our focus from the primacy of the architectural enclosure/envelope to that of interior-scaled architectural elements such as furniture, fixtures, and built-ins. As such, the project is organized by a set of contiguous, serpentine-shape, custom furniture pieces designed to facilitate new forms of working and learning.

Technology interfaces that are now compact, portable, or even integrated (such as computer monitors and hardware) were at this time overt, somewhat obtrusive elements. Institutions and businesses worldwide were confronted with (taking on) the challenges of integrating digital tools into workflows, both spatially and procedurally, yet most initial prototypes maintained the spatial traditions and hierarchies of predigital environments. Our design for Symonds aimed for innovative change in the spatial protocols of communication, research, and learning.

We have long considered spaces of production and exchange to be design precedents, and we routinely examine the spatial and organizational relationships that enable the creation of diverse workflows—involving people, material, tools, and information—over time. We recognize that consistent, discernable prioritization of shape and geometry in plan is necessary to facilitate, and even elicit, terms of engagement. For example, the radial arrangement of workers in historical glass blowing environments locates the shared heat source (fire) at the center of the space, allowing multiple participants to efficiently conduct work, individually and collaboratively, due to the visual and auditory connections articulated in plan. These connections, coupled with a single heat source, contribute to safety within the workspace while also allowing for the teaching and learning of craft processes among the artisans.

Our use of non-orthogonal shapes is not automatic but often motivated by the programmatic demands of a project. Geometry establishes measured spatial relationships that enable a range of anticipated and situational uses. In the Symonds Lab, a bold, curvilinear shape deployed in two dimensions organizes and mediates a diverse collection of physical, informational, and durational elements, setting up conditions of flexible collaboration in three dimensions. The serpentine-shape furniture pieces define the space and primary architectural contribution. They are detailed to integrate fixed equipment and to accommodate new forms of working and learning. The furniture pieces act as nodes within the open space and initiate collaborative engagement, positioning people through lines of sight (between students and teachers, whether seated or standing, and large-format screens, monitors, books, and maps), paths of movement (around and between objects), and audible connections (within and across the space). The complexity of the digital (and all that it implies) is tempered by organizing geometries in space to facilitate a range of activities.

Open Transfer

Open Transfer, our design proposal for a new light-rail platform in Houston, manages similarly collective, interactive architectural ambitions at the urban scale. The platform's three-block transfer zone, which occupies a slice of the city grid, requires passengers to use the public sidewalks to make connections between three rail lines. While bold in plan, the project touches lightly to the ground, setting up an implied new space of circulation that expands the given site.

The project positions an iconic object in the center of a street median in downtown Houston. The structure extends the length of a long, slender transit platform while spanning the street and connecting the sidewalks to form a monumental columnar threshold. The threshold implies a new public space connecting the sidewalks and street, while punctuating the transit platform. The organization of the urban object was derived from a comparative set of plan diagrams that we developed, titled Slim Fit and To the Point (see p 56–57). The former demonstrates the challenges of the existing conditions of circulation, directing crowds of people through standard, constricted crosswalks that run perpendicular to the platform median. The latter, which led to the final Open Transfer proposal, expands the space of pedestrian crossing radially to include more of the street, directing all pedestrian movement to one end of the platform. The organizational diagram shows a long narrow bar (the road median) with an intersecting circle (the new public space), biased toward one end of the bar. The architectural object is articulated and spatialized from this two-dimensional diagram to form the "spider column" threshold. Columns and canopy are designed and detailed to express a thin outer surface, as if the two-dimensional flat shape, first organized graphically and abstractly, were folded and extended to form the three supports and elevated structure. The simultaneous legibility of the original two-dimensional surface superimposed upon the three-dimensional object is an expression of architectural assembly found in many of our projects.

The outermost surface of the canopy structure is overlaid with a polychromatic, panelized rainscreen system assembled from recycled traffic signs. The vibrant surface, visible from the surrounding office towers and city sidewalks, renders the project a vivid icon in the urban context. However, when viewed from the platform, a solid white undersurface frames the surrounding block, collapsing the space of the platform, street, and sidewalk. These two distinct architectural experiences align the navigational and informational demands placed on public infrastructure with a more collective social ambition for the city.

Information—Shape

9° House

Client   Mark and Jenny Johnson
Dates   2006–2009
Location Houston, Texas

Every detail of the addition conforms to the nine-degree shift, making the interior transition between old and new architecture materially seamless and organizationally explicit through a striking experiential effect.

Located in an established, tree-lined neighborhood near downtown Houston, the 9° House occupies a more urban part of the city where residential and commercial areas, high-rise and mid-rise structures are all in close proximity. The street grid undulates in an S curve from east to west, while the property lines run perpendicular to the street's curvature, resulting in residential lots with unique geometric boundaries.

The existing house is a two-story bar-shape structure sited roughly parallel to the street and north property line. The new addition, which begins as a perpendicular bar, follows and aligns with the angled west property line. Connecting at the back edge of the existing house, the addition skews nine-degrees to fill the vacant southwest corner of the lot and expand the rear garden for outdoor activity. All walls oriented east–west in the addition remain parallel to the orthogonal geometry of the original house. All walls oriented north–south shift nine-degrees in plan, resulting in a sequence of parallelogram-shape spaces, built-in furniture, and stairs. Every detail of the addition conforms to the nine-degree shift, making the interior transition between old and new architecture materially seamless and organizationally explicit through a striking experiential effect. After spending time in the addition, the eye begins to compensate for the subtle effects of the unexpected geometries. Upon returning to the original wing of the house, the encounter with orthogonal spaces is momentarily destabilizing, slightly skewing the perceived shape of each room, presumably by nine-degrees, in the opposite direction.

A new exterior Swiss Pearl rainscreen panel system connects the old and new portions of the house, while allowing for formal and material distinctions between the two. The factory-machined warm-white panels wrap the upper portion of the original house, defined largely by one-story rough brick walls, a robust two-story chimney, and a built-in planter at the street front. The rainscreen panels envelop the addition at the front and sides, interrupted in two locations with large glass plug-on window assemblies and strategically perforated in three locations to allow diffuse light to reach the interior while maintaining privacy. A system of hardwood mahogany panels, doors, and frames with full-height glass connects the ground-level back elevations of the new and old structures, providing dynamic views across and through the private backyard.

First Level Plan

Renovation

1 Guest bedroom
2 Living room
3 Entry
4 Family room and dining

Addition

5 Side bar
6 Kitchen
7 Breakfast area
8 Laundry
9 Powder room
10 Master bedroom
11 Master bathroom
12 Master closet
13 Carport

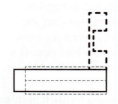

Demolition of existing one-story kitchen and carport.

New one-story addition shapes an exterior landscape facing the backyard.

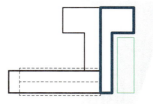

New two-story addition shapes an exterior hardscape facing the street.

Information—Shape

Second Level Plan

Renovation

14 Kid's bedroom 1
15 Kid's bedroom 2
16 Kid's bedroom 3

Addition

17 Plug-on at lounge area
18 Walkway/gallery
19 Study
20 Outdoor deck
21 (Future) green roof grid
22 Plug-on at stair

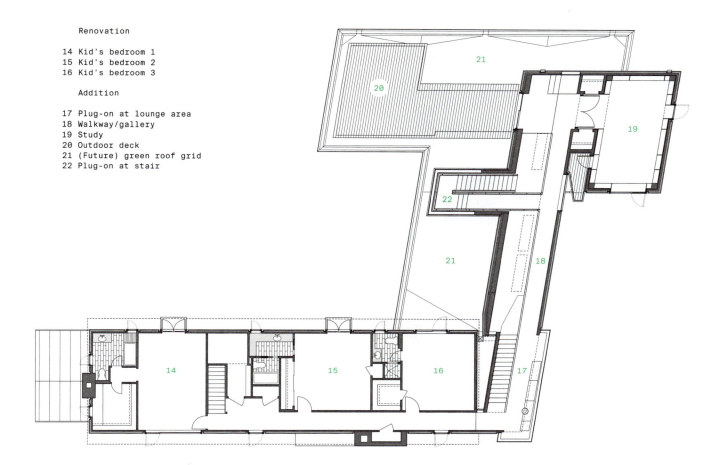

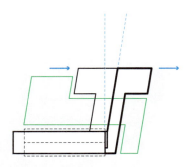

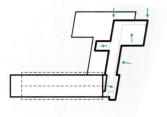

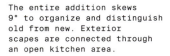

The entire addition skews 9° to organize and distinguish old from new. Exterior scapes are connected through an open kitchen area.

The two-story addition is modified and articulated to further engage domestic and urban activities.

9° House

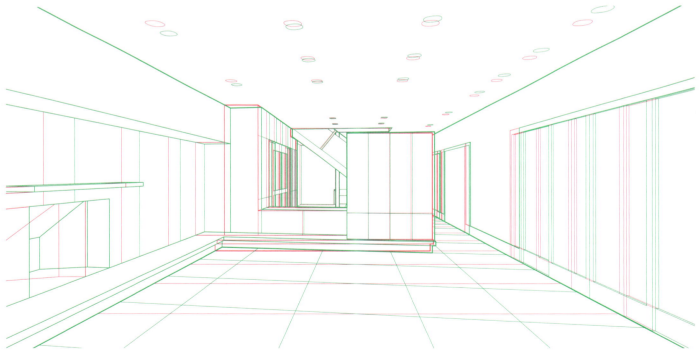

Perspective view of the orthogonal living room (in magenta) with a 9° shift drawing overlay (in green).

Drawing overlays demonstrate the geometric subtlety between old and new.

Information—Shape

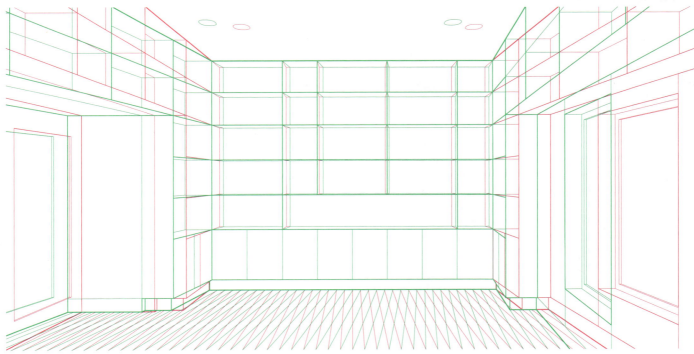

Perspective view of the 9° shifted study (in green) with an orthogonal drawing overlay (in magenta).

9° House

Existing brick base interlocks with new second-level exterior panels.

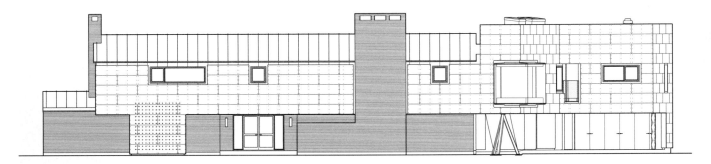

Front elevation

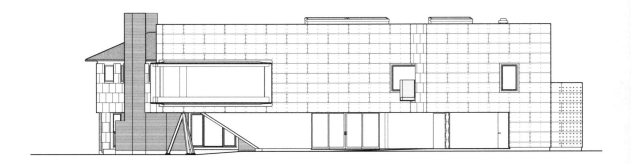

Side elevation

Stair

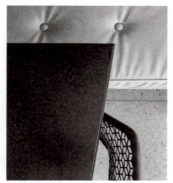
Banquette Seating

Downspout

Upholstered Bench

Terrazzo Aluminum Joint

Drawer

Rolled Tile Enclosure

Painted Steel Rail

Nakashima Mantel

Upholstered Column

Painted Steel Screen

Perforated Exterior Panels

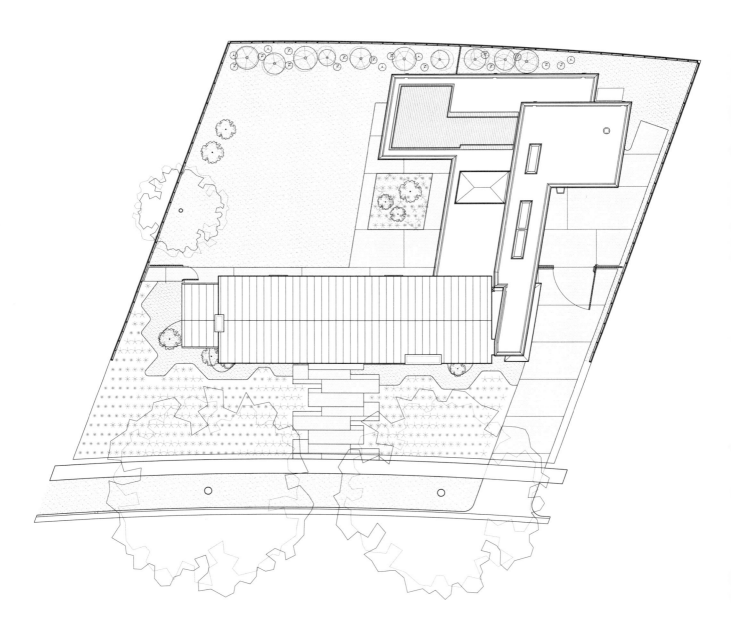

9° House

27

Two plug-on windows punctuate the ascent to the second level. The front plug-on, fitted with a custom leather upholstered bench and column, is visible from the street and marks the connection between old and new. A second, more private plug-on contains an open stair leading from the kitchen to the gallery walkway above.

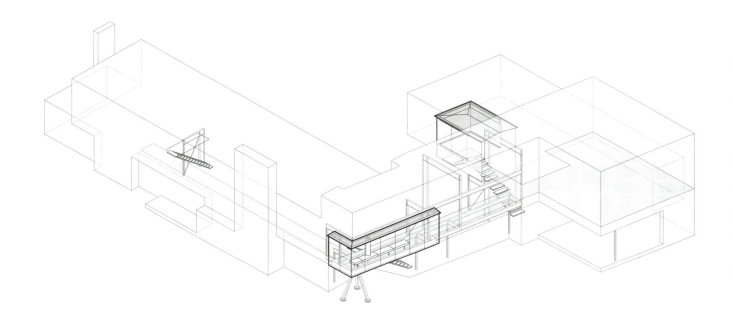

Three long, attenuated, open spaces follow the orthogonal and 9° axes of the house, punctuated with diffuse light that filters through perforated panels on the exterior.

1. The existing entry, living, and dining areas of the house were transformed to one main room that faces the rear private landscape.

2. A double-height volume and second-level gallery connect the upstairs bedrooms to a new study and exterior roof deck, providing visual and audible connections within the house.

3. An extended master suite space is organized in a gallery-like sequence of shower, vanity, closet, toilet, and bath.

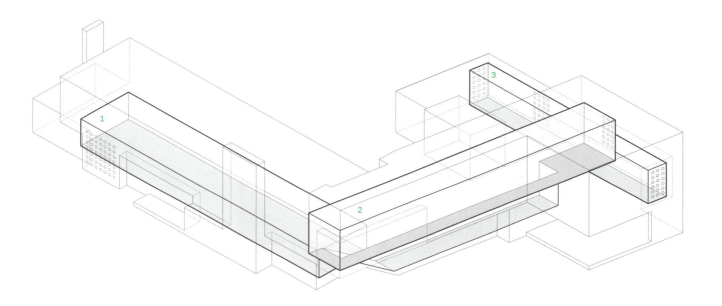

9° House

Architectural steel sets up an unobstructed, double-height space at the kitchen and gallery.

The forces accumulate and are stabilized by an exposed tripod column at the front corner of the house.

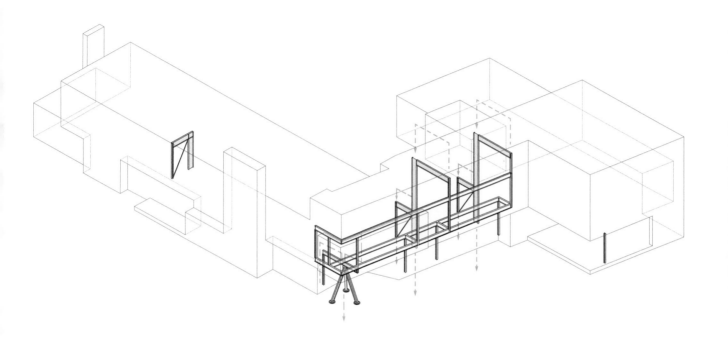

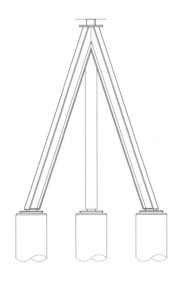

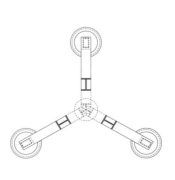

9° House

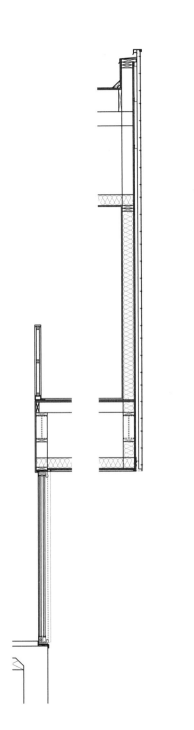
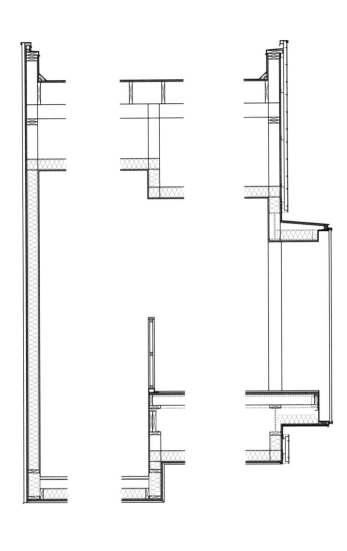

Wall sections at walkway, stair, and plug-on

Information—Shape

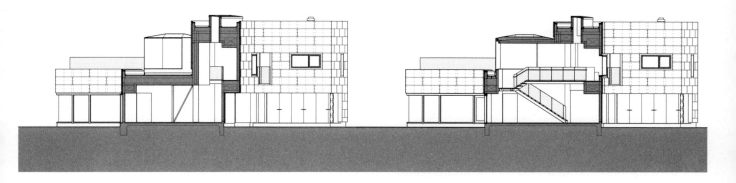

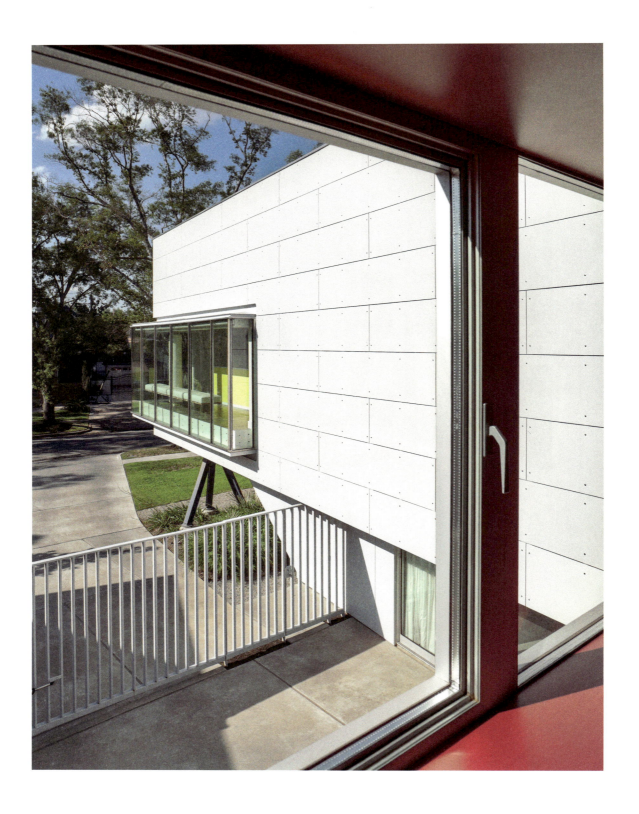

Symonds (+) Teaching Laboratories

Client	Rice University; Global Energy Corp.
Dates	1996, 2001, 2008
Location	Houston, Texas

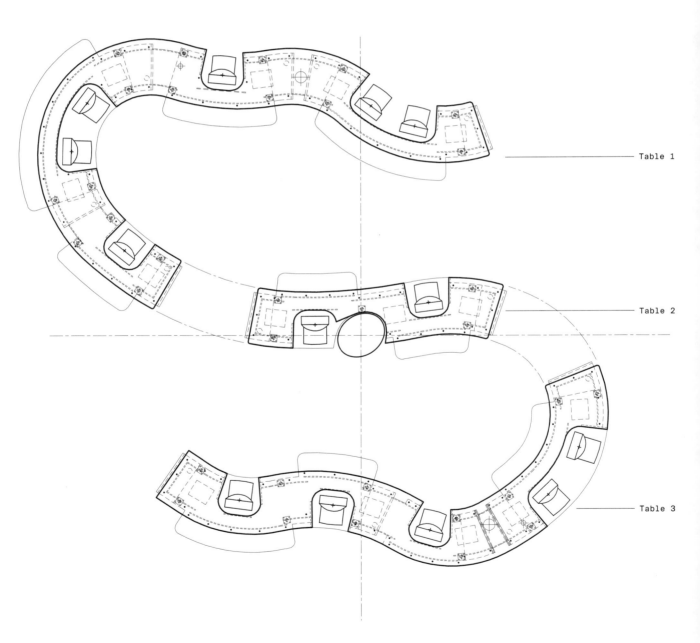

Table 1

Table 2

Table 3

Flexibility is embedded in the architecture but is latent, realized only by engagement.

In the late 1990s, we designed two experimental teaching classrooms with integrated digital technologies for teaching and research at Rice University in Houston. Our proposals abandoned the one-to-one computer-to-user convention in favor of a more collaborative, ergonomic, and dynamic solution. Custom furniture and architectural fixtures were designed to amplify the integration of diverse new technologies and to reshape working and learning methods. Simple, legible geometries were carefully developed in plan and constructed as furniture, lighting, and acoustic panels to elicit, in three dimensions, subtle but important relationships between people, information, tools, and space. Flexibility is embedded in the architecture but is latent, realized only by engagement.

Sited in the existing central library on campus, the first Gardiner Symonds Teaching Laboratory comprises two adjoining spaces: a multimedia classroom and a breakout conference room for video teleconference services. The main classroom space is defined by a large serpentine-shape furniture piece, segmented to form smaller work areas with implied spatial and operative connections. The classroom incorporates two rear-screen projectors, an overhead video projector, an audience camera, a resource area with flat-bed scanners and printers, and, perhaps most important, one personal computer for every two students. Ample surface area is provided for the cooperative referencing of maps, books, computer screens, and other research articles. The serpentine-shape desks establish multiple, simultaneous lines of sight and sound, prompting collaborative discussion, the sharing of information, and interaction over time.

This and other teaching laboratory studies led to further commissions from a global energy corporation in need of specialized classrooms for the teaching of proprietary, immersive digital learning protocols and for navigating real-time national and global emergencies. Our three proposals, Tri-pod, Switchback, and Mono-fold, build upon our earlier research and have been implemented around the globe. More advanced and compact than Symonds, the technological components of these three classrooms presented ergonomic demands of greater complexity, leading to a collection of robust shapes in plan to address the various durational needs of diverse new teaching models.

Phase Space and Physical
Space Diagrams

Peripherals

Local
Workstations

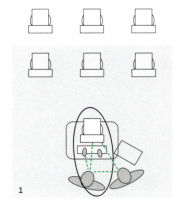 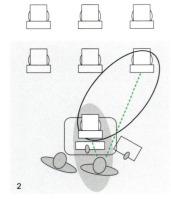 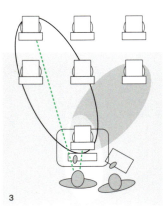

Phase Space

First-level computer interface between users and workstation.

Second-level computer interface between multiple user workstations within physical classroom environment.

Third-level computer interface between user workstations and network users.

Peripherals

Local
Workstations

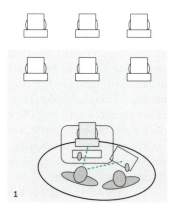 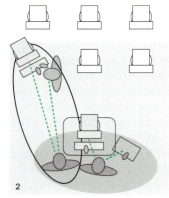 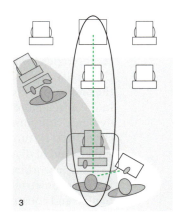

Physical Space

First-level physical interface between users and workspaces.

Second-level physical interface between multiple user workspaces within physical classroom environment.

Third-level physical interface between user workspaces and peripherals.

Information—Shape

Custom serpentine-shape desks

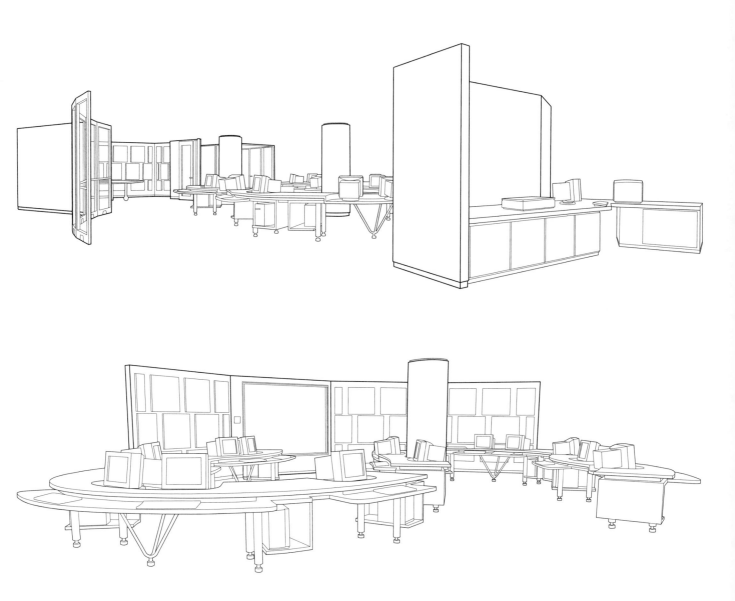

Symonds (+) Teaching Laboratories

Plan and Reflected
Ceiling Plan

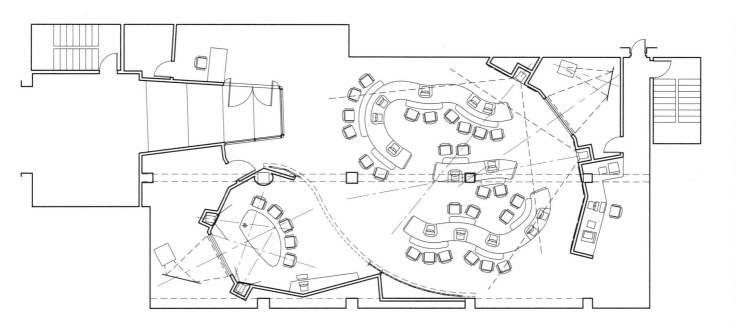

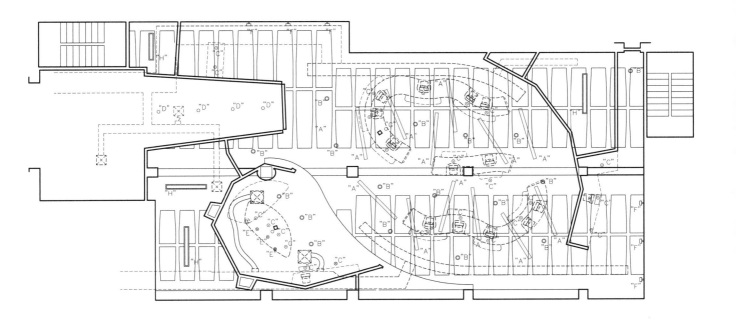

Symonds (+) Teaching Laboratories 43

Symonds (+) Teaching Laboratories

Tri-pod

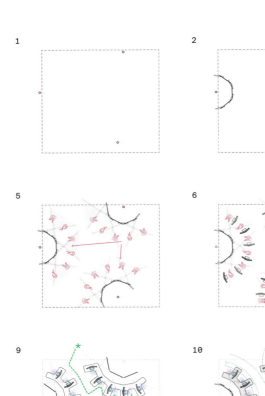
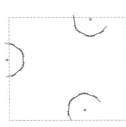
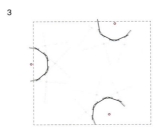

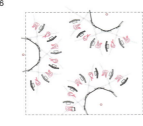

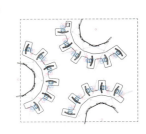
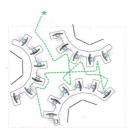
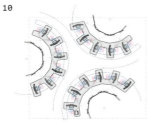
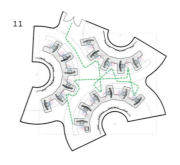
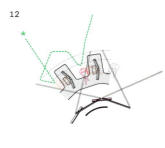

Sequence Diagrams

1   Introduce three focal points at perimeter of room.

2   Array a series of 72" displays and 46" displays at each focal point.

3   Orient displays outward, away from focal points.

4   Position students toward displays and in relation to one another around three focal points.

5   Provide unobstructed views between focal points and remote displays.

6   Position workstations adjacent to each student and at an angle to displays.

7   Allow room for students to rotate away from displays and toward workstations.

8   Shape furniture around this motion.

9   Free corridors for movement between the three "pods" for instructor supervision and contact.

10 Graphically punctuate the furniture shapes.

11 Reinforce the functionality of the room with development of ceiling and wall architecture.

12 Exchange information. Work and learn.

Information—Shape

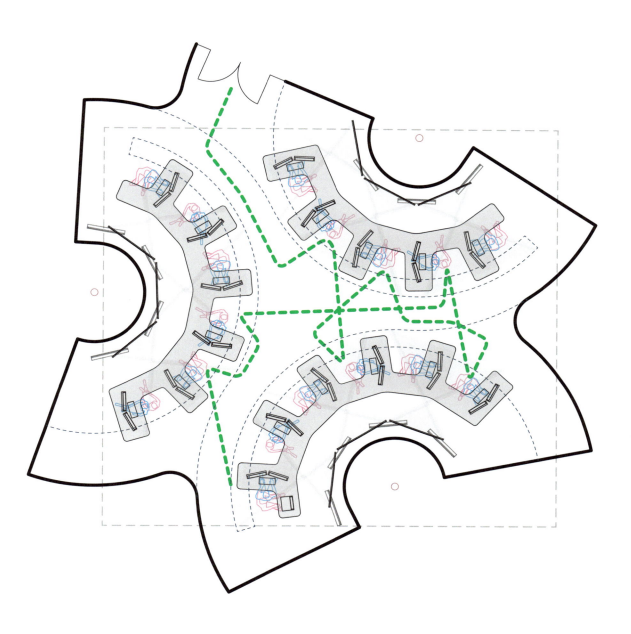

Symonds (+) Teaching Laboratories

Switchback

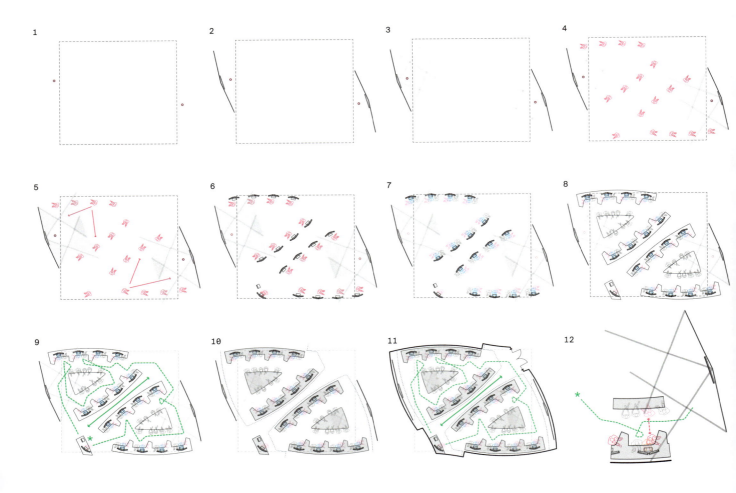

Sequence Diagrams

1 Introduce two focal points at either end of room.

2 Position two pairs of front projection 6' x 12' displays, one at each focal point.

3 Orient displays across room, away from focal points.

4 Position students toward displays and in relation to two open-view corridors.

5 Provide unobstructed views to focal points and across view corridors.

6 Position workstations adjacent to each student and at an angle to displays.

7 Allow room for each student to rotate away from displays and toward workstations.

8 Shape furniture around this motion. Add table at center of each view corridor for breakout sessions.

9 Free corridors for movement between the two view corridors for instructor supervision and contact.

10 Graphically punctuate the furniture shapes.

11 Reinforce the functionality of the room with development of ceiling and wall architecture.

12 Exchange information. Work and learn.

Information—Shape

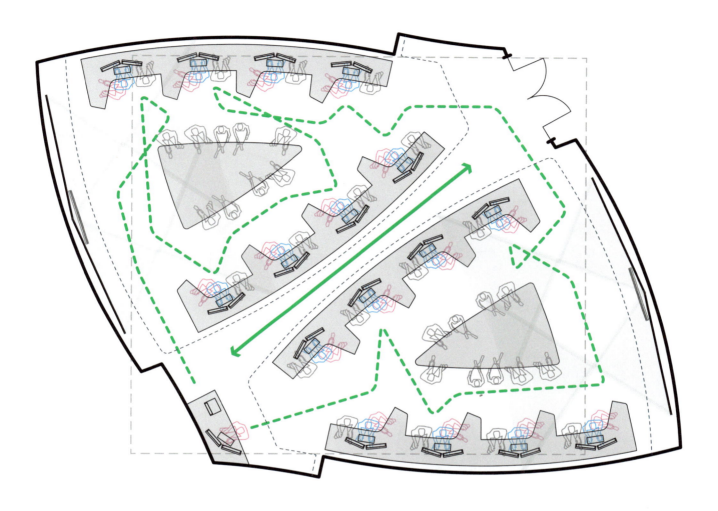

Symonds (+) Teaching Laboratories

Mono-fold

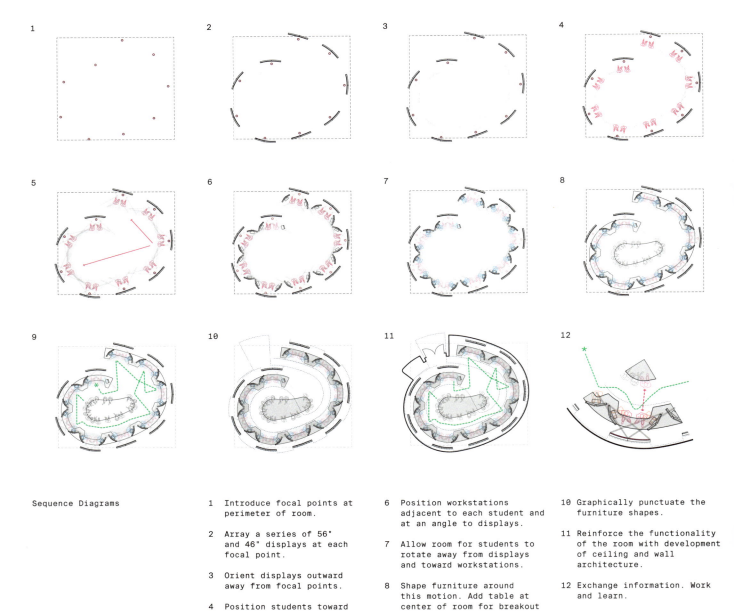

Sequence Diagrams

1. Introduce focal points at perimeter of room.
2. Array a series of 56" and 46" displays at each focal point.
3. Orient displays outward away from focal points.
4. Position students toward displays in pairs.
5. Provide unobstructed views between focal points and remote displays.
6. Position workstations adjacent to each student and at an angle to displays.
7. Allow room for students to rotate away from displays and toward workstations.
8. Shape furniture around this motion. Add table at center of room for breakout session.
9. Free corridors for movement between perimeter table and center table for instructor supervision and contact.
10. Graphically punctuate the furniture shapes.
11. Reinforce the functionality of the room with development of ceiling and wall architecture.
12. Exchange information. Work and learn.

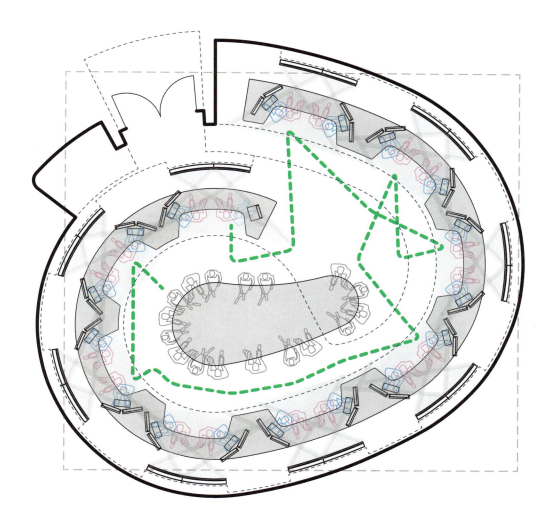

Symonds (+) Teaching Laboratories

Open Transfer

Client	Houston METRO, Houston Rapid Transit, & HDMD
Dates	2012
Location	Houston, Texas

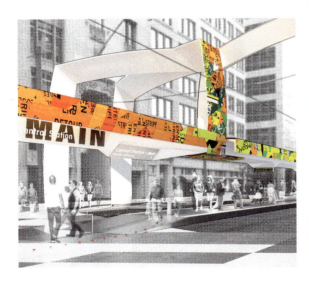

52 Information—Shape

The canopy generates two distinct, simultaneous visual experiences mediated through the superimposition of form and surface.

Houston's transit infrastructure is rapidly expanding to serve diverse neighborhoods in the city. Three new light-rail lines will intersect in downtown Houston at a new transfer zone that occupies not only the city grid but also the public right of way. Riders will have to use sidewalks and streets to make connections between trains and buses. To generate public support and publicity for the rail project, an invited national competition was held in 2012 for the design of one light-rail platform and canopy. The site is a narrow eleven-foot-eight-inch-wide median dividing four lanes of vehicular traffic and extending the full length of one city block.

Open Transfer proposes a new threshold in the city, defined by a monumental "spider" column hovering above one end of the long platform, spanning and visually framing Main Street. Two of the spider's three legs converge above a slender canopy to support a long-span truss. The effect is an open view that visually expands the space of the platform to include the street and sidewalk. All movement through the site—including pedestrians, bikers, trains, buses, and private vehicles—is through the threshold, since all modes of transport share the transfer zone.

The canopy assembly is a large architectural object positioned to reshape and expand the space of the narrow platform. It generates two distinct, simultaneous visual experiences mediated through the super-imposition of form and surface. The canopy's outer surface, or exterior cladding, consists of polychromatic panels made of recycled aluminum traffic signs. Visible from the sidewalk and from the surrounding mid-rise buildings, the thin layer of saturated colors and composite patterns presents a compelling public icon. Viewed from within the platform, or from an approaching vehicle, the color and form recede as the white elastomeric undersurface frames the collective streetscape, highlighting the expansive urban space of the transfer station. The project registers and makes legible the tension and coincidence between the two-dimensional graphic surface and the three-dimensional object shape while exposing the complex material assemblies that are coordinated in the architecture.

Each year in the United States thousands of road signs are discarded after being damaged in accidents or weather-related events or are decommissioned because of roadway changes and upgrades. The composite road signs are made of a UV-resistant laminate material adhered to a one-eighth-inch aluminum sheet. They are almost impossible to recycle, as the laminate cannot be easily removed from the aluminum. In Open Transfer their use as an architectural cladding material references the dominance of automobile culture in Houston's recent past and marks a new urban investment in the design of public transportation infrastructures.

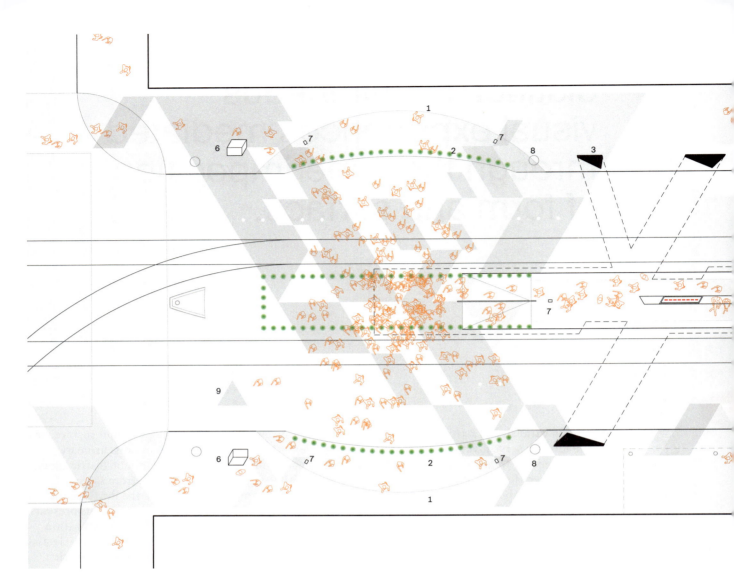

N

1 Open platform dish
2 Embedded compact LED "STOP" and "GO" indicators
3 Structural spider column
4 Seating, signage, system maps
5 Structural plate column
6 Ticket vending machines
7 Existing OCS poles
8 Ticket validators
9 Ground surface paving

Information—Shape

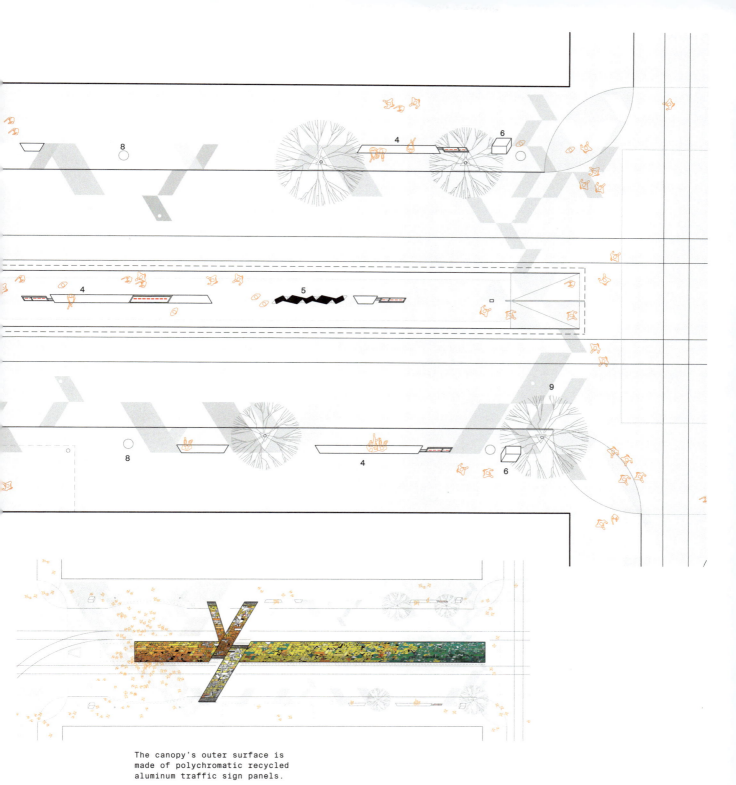

The canopy's outer surface is made of polychromatic recycled aluminum traffic sign panels.

Open Transfer

Slim Fit

The existing narrow platform serves two-way rail traffic with pedestrian crosswalks at either end. This configuration required the platform to be densely packed with signage, ticket vending machines, validators, and seating.

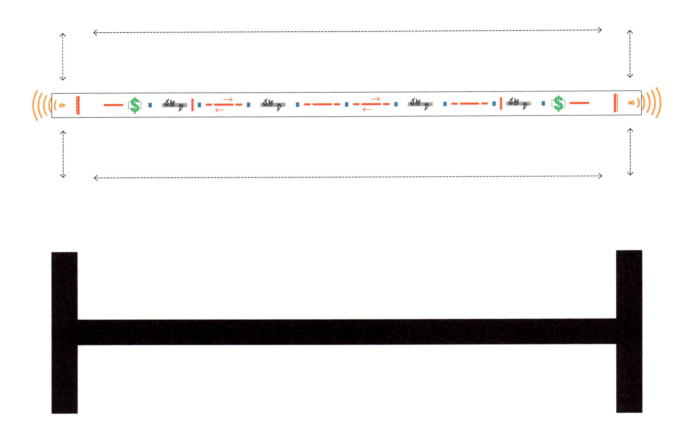

56   Information—Shape

To the Point

Open Transfer proposes that the southern end of the platform open and expand to engage the space of the street. This revised circulation path relocates the transverse crosswalks at each end of the platform to the center of the block, directing movement across the street from a single point.

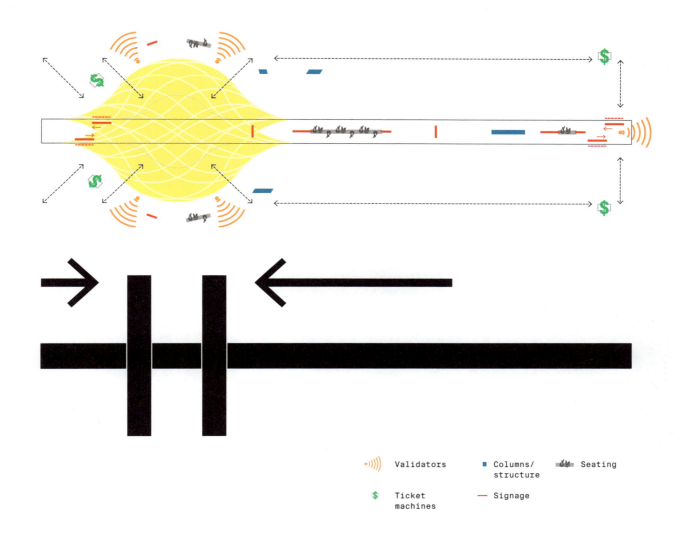

-)))) Validators   ■ Columns/   ▃▃ Seating
                           structure

$ Ticket   — Signage
      machines

Open Transfer   57

View from an oncoming train (above) and from the open center of the platform (below)

Information—Shape

Two of the spider column legs converge above the canopy to support a long-span truss. By displacing the column supports to the sidewalk, the space of the platform visually expands to the street and sidewalk.

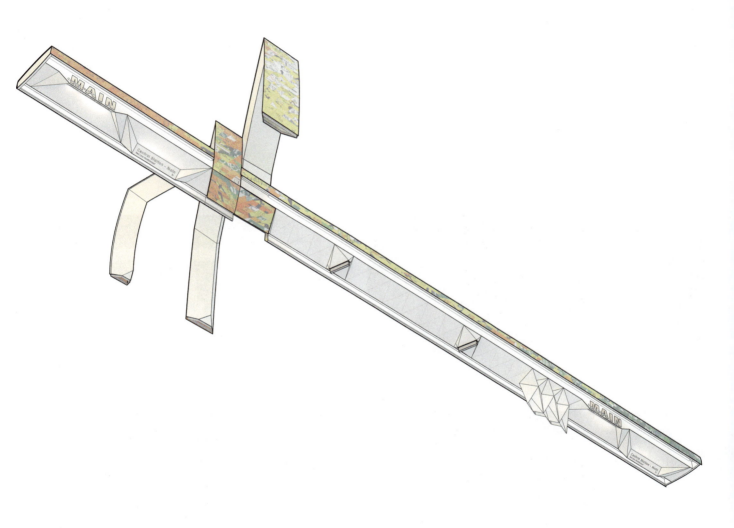

Open Transfer

Section Renderings

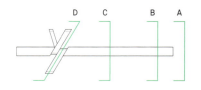

Information—Shape

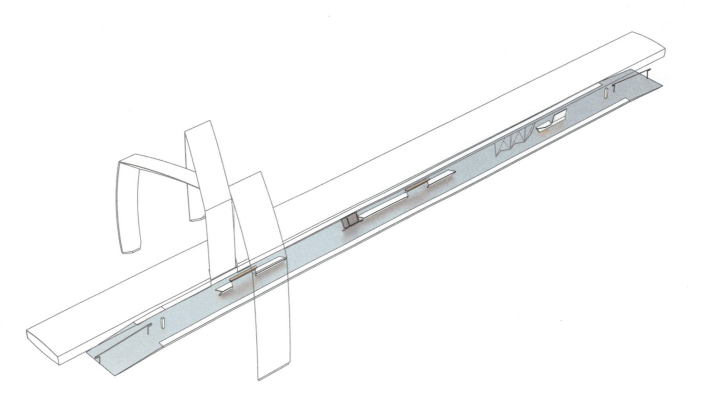

A triangulated steel truss structure makes up the spanning and cantilevered portions of the canopy.

Information—Shape

The structure is shop fabricated into eleven manageable components for assembly and delivery to the site.

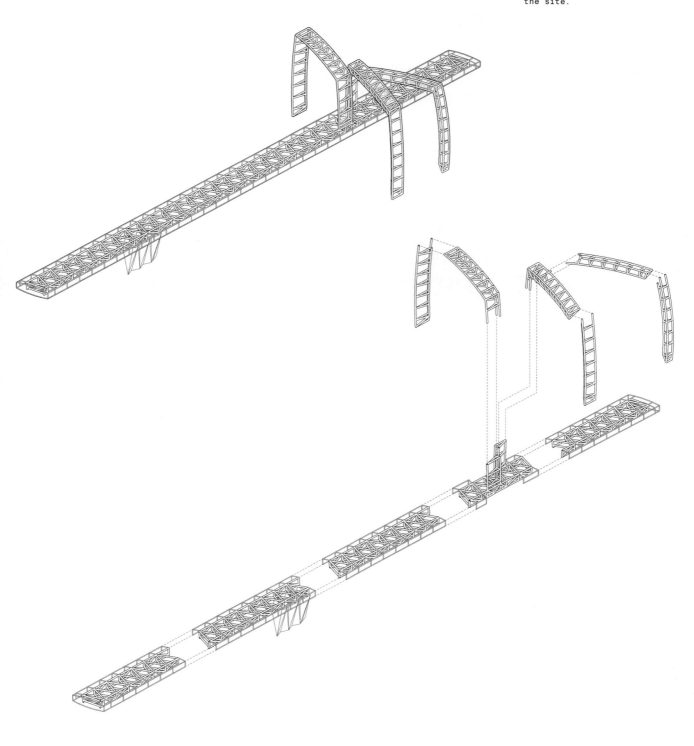

Open Transfer

View from sidewalk

64 Information—Shape

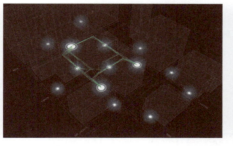
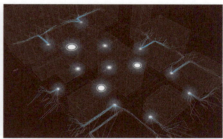

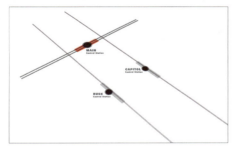
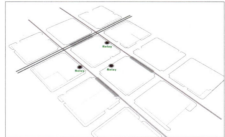
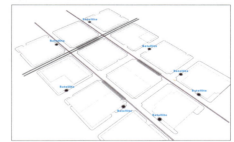

The transfer zone between and beyond the three downtown platforms is supported with wayfinding points and satellite information kiosks (left to right).

Open Transfer

Collection and
Preparation

Used traffic signs are collected from local, city, and state highway yards. Panels are cut from each sign based upon a pre-determined pattern and the given color. Edges are cleaned and de-burred. Panels are then formed and rolled to ensure an even surface. Holes are drilled for exposed aluminum pop-rivet fasteners and a UV resistant sealer is sprayed over the panel to extend the life of the laminate and prevent oxidation.

66 Information—Shape

Pattern and Surface

Panels are then numbered to correspond to their place in the pattern. When the structure is sheathed and sealed, and the lightweight aluminum panels are installed, the panels are laid up and pop-riveted with 0.25" open joints in between. The traffic panels form a gradient color band, transitioning from green (north edge) to yellow to orange (south edge).

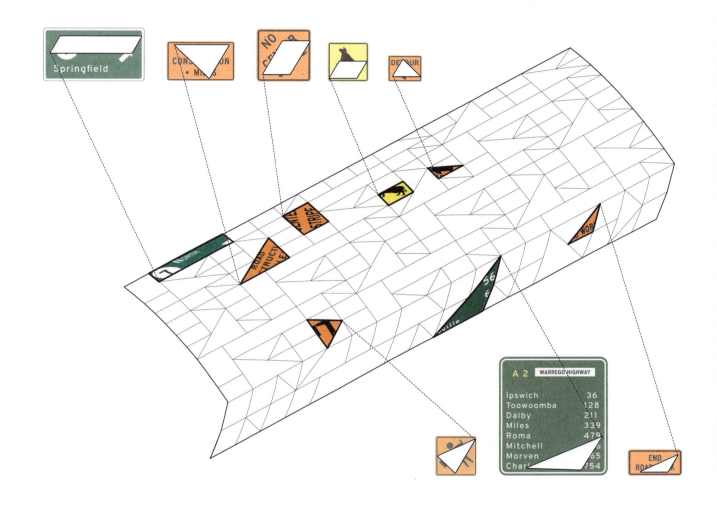

Open Transfer

67

Material Assembly

1 Cut aluminum rainscreen panels
2 Lightweight aluminum hat channels
3 Adhesive-backed, self-healing, foil-faced waterproof membrane
4 Composite sheathing
5 Triangulated canopy structure
6 Drainage and power infrastructure
7 Formed aluminum gutter
8 Modified acrylic cement on mesh, integral color

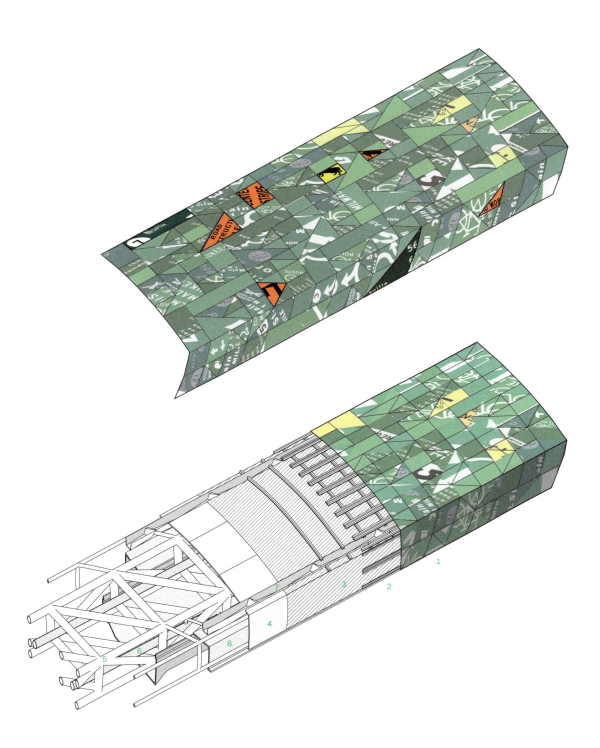

Information—Shape

Canopy Components

Eleven prefabricated members are shop assembled with rain-screen enclosure assembly and canopy soffit. These assembled components are loaded onto a standard semi trailer for site delivery and installation.

Delivery of prefabricated/preassembled canopy components allows for efficient installation on-site with minimal disruption to downtown transit.

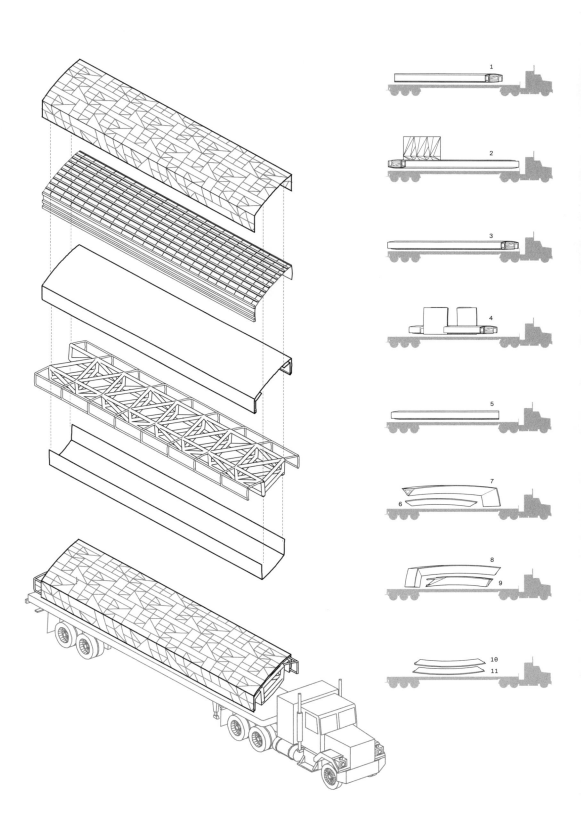

Cut aluminum rainscreen panels

Lightwight aluminum hat channels

Commercial grade sheathing with adhesive-backed, self-healing, foil-faced waterproof membrane

Triangulated canopy structure (with drainage and power infrastructure and formed aluminum gutter)

Modified acrylic cement on mesh, integral color

Open Transfer

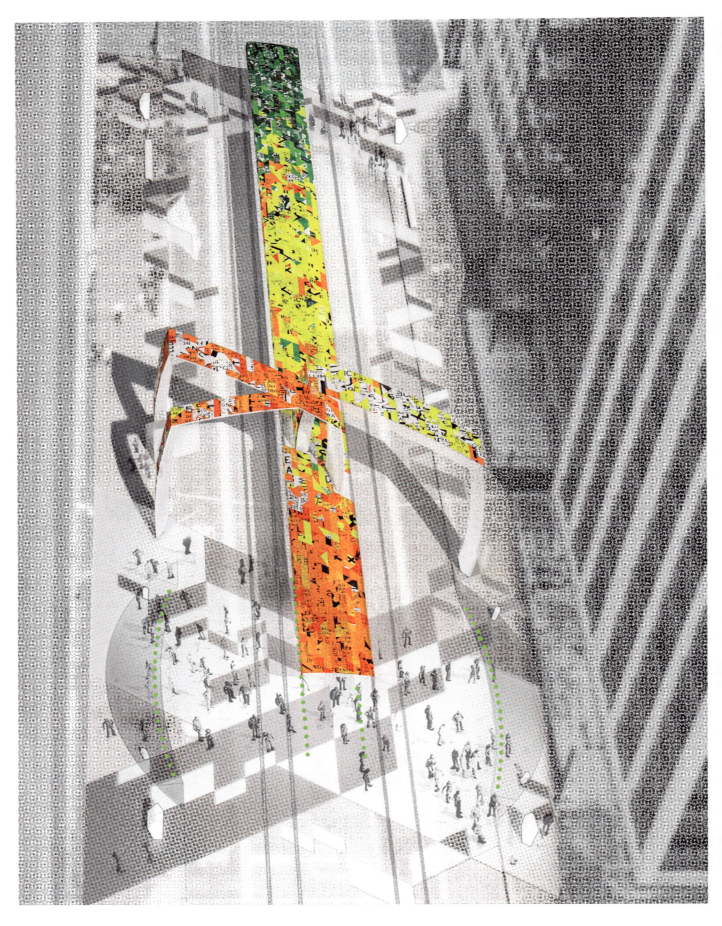

Information—Shape

Composed Surface

The open-joint system allows water to drain through to the membrane surface, then across to the integral roof drain system.

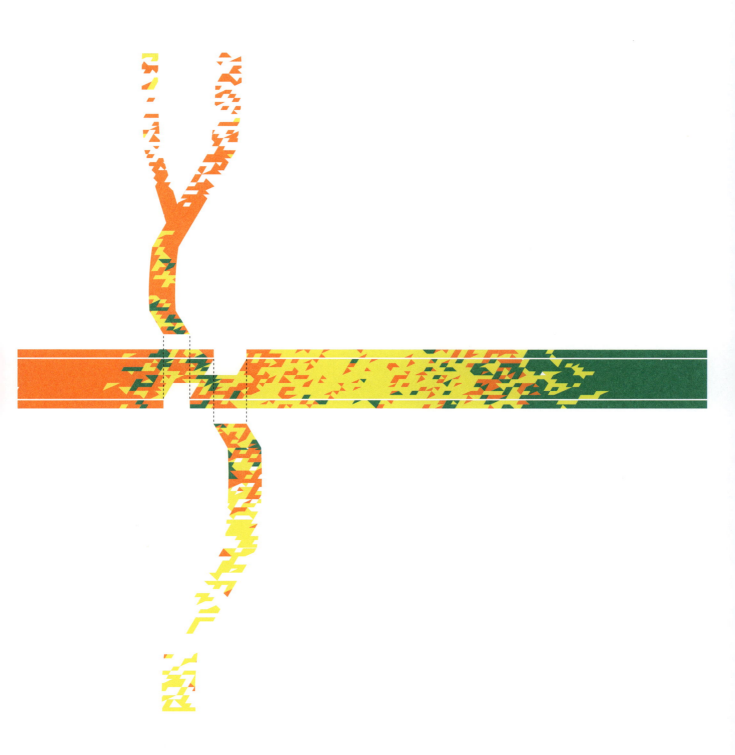

Open Transfer

Notes No. 1

A system is a collection of interacting components, with arbitrary boundaries, that enable activities to be performed.

1.01 Diagramming Information

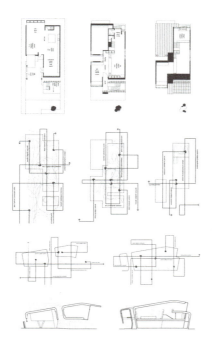

Historically, architects have been engaged primarily with the practice of drawing, a two-dimensional medium used to represent and explore the physical and material properties of buildings. This practice expanded in the late twentieth century to include new representational types and formats that allow architects to mediate, organize, and communicate the physical, procedural, and temporal aspects of architecture within the additional constraints of our new digital culture.

The Houston Products Lab building was designed in 1997 for a specialty design-fabrication company in Houston. To study the complex processes of material and information exchange required in the workspace, both digital and analog, we developed abstract products and information exchange diagrams that identify the distinct information formats being transferred and the spatial or nonspatial conditions of each. These diagrams led to a new distribution of program, not through defined rooms but as sets of fluid activities. Diagrams describe how people, products, and information are organized by and operate through business practice routines, equipment, and architecture.

1.02 Intensive Environments

We often study existing spaces of material practice and production, specifically to evaluate how precise spatial/organizational relationships structure efficient, simultaneous workflows among people, materials, tools, and information over time. We refer to these spaces as *intensive environments* and note how their plans prioritize shape and geometry to facilitate, and even elicit, terms of engagement.

Examples include the radial organization of workers surrounding a heat source in historical glass blowing environments or the field-like organization of stock market and casino spaces that manage large groups of people with the streaming of simultaneous visual and audio data in relation to space. Open spaces enable dynamic interactions to take place over time, within a distributed field of proto-architectural furniture and built-ins that are geometrically articulated in plan.

1.03 (Un)Built-Ins

Notes No. 1   73

In the 9° House, several custom built-in cabinets separate and support discrete functions within the domestic interior while generating visual, social, and functional overlaps between activities. The black, object-like U-shape kitchen cabinet separates and synthesizes cooking and food preparation, along with dining, kids' homework, and outdoor patio play. The cabinet is located in the center of the kitchen space and is detailed to appear neither completely built-in nor free-standing but to call attention to its organizational significance within the space.

1.04   Nakashima Mantel

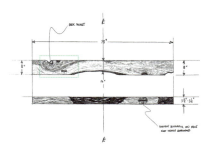

We worked with George Nakashima Woodworkers to design a custom fireplace mantel for the main living room of the 9° House. Nakashima's daughter, Mira, who took over the Japanese woodcraft business after her father's death in 1990, provided us with specifications for our small, unique object. In the design process, shape was not abstractly projected upon material but derived from the available potential of raw, unique slabs of fibrous organic hardwoods (walnut and rosewood) harvested for their enduring quality and aesthetic character. The drawings and communication exchange required for the fabrication of this precise Nakashima piece relied on the subjective selection, experience, and judgment of a craftsperson.

1.05   Wrapped Column and Bench

In the 9° House, the location of an interior steel column punctuates the juncture of the old and new portions of the house and performs a critical structural function for the double-height family space. Upholstered in leather with a thick, padded infill, the ambiguous vertical built-in reframes a necessary structural object (the column) as a site for playful interaction (it resembles a punching bag). Intended to protect the young children of the household as they slide around the corner chasing one another in play, the leather enclosure is detailed with stainless steel grommets and leather binding cord—a clear reference to the punching bags used in boxing. The accompanying custom bench with reflective chrome legs appears to float outward from the column, offering a space of rest, perfect for a rainy day.

1.06   House on Avalon Place

Located on Avalon Place near downtown Houston, the original house was designed and built in 1955 by architects Wilson, Morris, Crain and Anderson, who in 1960 designed the world's first domed stadium, the Houston Astrodome. Robust, abstract volumes of both the interior and exterior house were detailed with traditional adornment and materials, a curious combination of styles. For example, the main living space had elaborate crown molding overlaid with a rational, International Style floor plan and large custom steel and glass sliding doors opening to the back lawn. When the house was renovated, this eclectic sensibility was maintained through the application of vibrant paint colors, the addition of custom built-in cabinetry, and the installation of a collection of idiosyncratic objects and furniture owned by the clients.

1.07   Pool Scape

Pool Scape is an extensive residential landscape project that completes the 9° House. The overall landscape strategy uses a two-dimensional pentagram as a repetitive graphic organizer. Six pentagrams of varying size define six zones for backyard leisure (one a wood deck for lounging, one a planted garden, one a paved dining area, and three that together form deep, shallow, and tanning-shelf areas of a pool). The collection of shapes is densely packed, each zone aligned to at least one edge of another pentagram, often slipping past one another to form secondary, in-between spaces for additional gravel and planting beds.

   Our work included collaboration with a horticulturist to develop native plant microecologies that attract local bees, lizards, and butterflies. The gardens contain a diverse array of plants that surround and buffer the pool.

1.08   Green Room

Notes No. 1   75

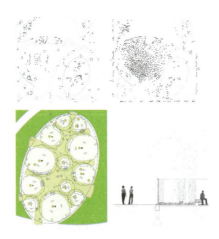

Green Room is one architectural element within a schematic design for a vacant courtyard on the Rice University campus in Houston. The aim of the project is to support a range of formal and informal student activities. The design overlays a series of curvilinear geometries in plan, materialized with trees, plantings, paving, and minimal construction to reshape the existing blank lawn into small and medium spaces for study and recreation.

    A translucent screen/wall encloses an oval cluster of trees, producing an open room within the courtyard. Fixed benches are located along the crushed granite paths and plantings within the outdoor room, allowing individuals and groups to socialize or study in the shade. Shape and material provide varying levels of visual privacy while maintaining visual connections to critical areas of the courtyard and commons.

1.09   Reiss House

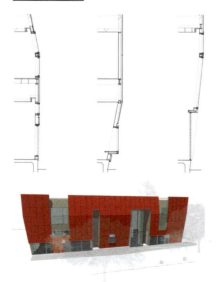

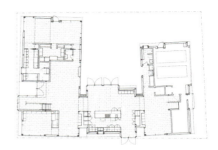

This new single-family residence is sited on a large corner lot in Houston, within a neighborhood developed in the early 1900s. While geometry is prioritized in plan for the 9° House, the Reiss House combines a subtle manipulation of geometry in plan with a more overt skewing of geometry in section. In plan, geometry is used to organize and separate program. In section, geometry is used to visually connect and spatially direct activity. The house is developed as three discrete constructed volumes that enclose an implied fourth volume. Two outer volumes rotate two degrees and minus two degrees respectively toward a shared outdoor space, while bracketing an orthogonal double-height family space between. The exterior facade surfaces are graphically linked through facets that visually and spatially connect the three building volumes.

1.10   Welch Street House

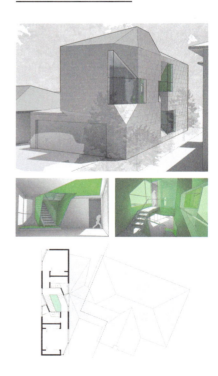

Welch Street House is a compact yet spatially expansive addition to a pristine single-family residence in Houston, originally constructed in 1945. The slender addition includes a family leisure space,

Information—Shape

laundry, and garage at the ground level, with one kid's bedroom, a connecting bathroom, and a master suite above.

Like the 9° House, the addition shifts away from the original house, following the geometry of the unique lot shape. Specific cuts in the new building mass and facade follow and mirror the original house's orthogonal grid to introduce spatial relief. These angles organize the geometry of the central stairway and the flow of vertical circulation.

The central open stairway serves as a social link between private bedrooms (staggered at half-levels to one another), radically repositioning the more public aspects of domestic space. Hand sinks, coat racks, built-in dressers, and benches are seamlessly integrated within the stair volume as a reflection of the more common daily habits shared by families.

1.11   Publication

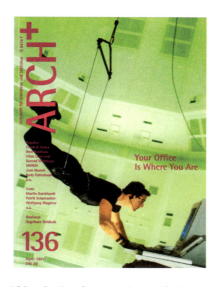

Issue 136 of the German journal *Arch+* (1997), "Your Office Is Where You Are," features the Gardiner Symonds Teaching Laboratory and a collection of experimental intensive information environments installed worldwide.

1.12   Studies of Teaching and Learning

Rice University used a grant from the Culpepper Foundation to assign the management and operation of the Gardiner Symonds Laboratory to data librarian Doralyn H. Edwards and Adjunct Associate Professor of Psychology Janice Bordeaux. Bordeaux conducted exhaustive studies of teaching and learning by observing, sketching, and interviewing the students and faculty who use the lab space. Her academic findings endorsed the nonhierarchical architectural organization designed to elicit collaboration and to coordinate digital technologies, audiovisual communication, and physical artifacts within new spaces of instruction. Her findings also prompted Rice University to commission an "Instructional Technologies" study for the campus and a second technology laboratory, Symonds II.

1.13   Instructional Technologies and Scenarios

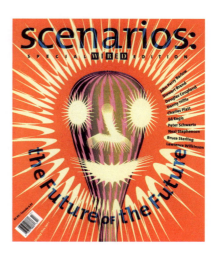

Notes No. 1   77

In 1997, Rice University commissioned our office to study and visualize the impact of information technology, shifts in teaching practice, and new organizational concepts on the delivery of higher education. We developed a long-term scenario planning method for campus building and classroom design and speculated about how the integration of audiovisual, multimedia technologies might transform university research and teaching over time.

In the 1990s, Lawrence Wilkinson of Global Business Network developed *scenario planning*, a method for navigating future uncertainty in business. "The future is certain, but what it carries with it is not. Nevertheless, actions have to be taken today that will play out in uncertain ways tomorrow. Through scenario planning, plausible futures can be mapped out so that as features of a future actually begin to play out, relationships that would also follow from that future might be avoided if they are detrimental, or pursued if they are desirable." We adapted this pragmatic and projective method, which was outlined in a 1995 *Wired* magazine article entitled "How to Build Scenarios," to our own practice protocols to reinforce our position that architecture is produced and resides within the complex processes of the world.

Our renovation of the student center at the University of Houston Downtown Campus in 1998 animated the rigid orthogonal layout of the existing interior through plan-generated figures and shapes. These shapes reconfigure and facilitate the flow of administrators and students engaging in university tasks such as enrollment, registration, and counseling, as well as more social, student-led activities conducted by clubs, academic teams, and community outreach groups. The formal and the programmatic, that is, converge to support academic operations, communication, wayfinding, and social encounters. The shapes remain open and accessible, defined graphically by color (paint), ceiling soffits, tile pattern, and perforated vertical screens that support counters and shelves while partially screening adjacent spaces. The original concrete structure and orthogonal layout of the interior remain legible so as to highlight departmental distinctions, which are generated through shape and color.

1.14   Departmental Figures

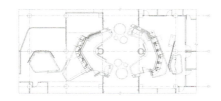

1.15   Perth Amboy High School (PAHS)

78   Information—Shape

Our design research of working and learning environments continued through the (radical scale shift) design of a new 500,000-square-foot high school in Perth Amboy, New Jersey for an open national competition. Our proposal for a forward-thinking public facility acknowledges spatial and operational aspects of the building that will continue to perform long after the architects, engineers and planners have disengaged from the process. As with all public schools, PAHS will evolve under the direction of educators, administrators, parents, community forces, business leaders, and students; all the beneficiaries of our endeavor.

1.16 Arrays and Accumulations

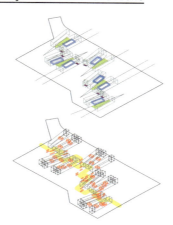

We designated portions of the PAHS building to be infrastructural, with spaces—called "arrays"—that remain physically constant but operationally dynamic. Arrays are basic building elements arranged serially according to departmental requirements. They are rationalized, contained spaces made up of academic branches, courtyards, and instructional commons.

We designated other portions of the building to evolve physically in accordance with spatial needs that arise over time. These spatial needs are the result of collaborative events involving diverse program sponsors, educational leaders, researchers, intellectuals, and thinkers, and are called "accumulations." Accumulations are dynamic, event-generated spaces that support sponsored programs initiated by students, instructors, administrators, private industry advocates, and parents.

Together, arrays and accumulations provide the school administration with a strategy for planning a vital building while acknowledging open-ended future circumstances that are impossible to predict yet necessary to anticipate. We expect that advanced institutional facilities will be required to perform much like intelligent organisms, absorbing and processing internal issues while engaging, influencing, and shaping the environment and context around them.

1.17 Scenario Strategy

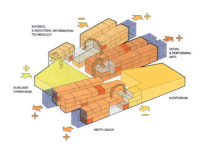

Education is a system calibrated to enrich those within it by immersing them in a set of diverse, energetic, cross-reacting influences. These forces are at times traditional and predictable; at other times they surprise and enlighten. We believe PAHS will maintain an inclusive philosophy and broad strategy for coordinating local and global program sponsors. Our design architecturally promotes and manages the diverse internal and external alliances in public education by projecting spatial and operational scenarios for what collaborations could happen at PAHS between the auditorium, ninth grade, the auxiliary gymnasium, the Business and Industrial Information Technology Academy, and the Visual and Performing Arts Academy. This scenario situates plausible futures to illustrate the operational dynamic that must ensue with any environment of quality given the inevitability and need for change.

1.18 Boundary Objects

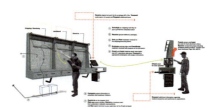

Object 1

Object 2

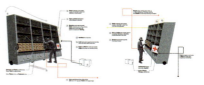

Object 3

Notes No. 1

In the Houston Products Lab, adjacent spaces and their respective activities are organized around eight *boundary objects*. Boundary objects are strategically located, functionally diverse pieces of built-in furniture that accommodate aspects of the business by organizing spaces where one activity overlaps another. The shape, position, orientation, and material of each object is calibrated to accommodate ergonomic and procedural criteria. Each piece facilitates specified workflows while supporting social encounters, shared resources, or associated interests.

Object 1: Job Board (check-in, shipping, and receiving) located on ground floor between fabrication and set-up

Object 2: Reception (display, making, labeling, and packaging) located on second floor between conference and design

Object 3: Rolling Work Wall (sorting, stocking, and receiving) located on ground floor between fabrication and materials

1.19   Aluminum by Design

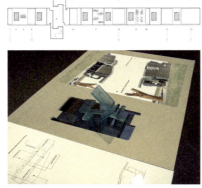

The Houston Products Lab was presented at the Heinz Architectural Center's *Aluminum in Contemporary Architecture* exhibition at the Carnegie Museum of Art, Pittsburgh. Our office designed and fabricated a sixteen-foot-long narrow table to display drawings, diagrams, models, and renderings. A steel, powder-coated frame supports nine custom-milled aluminum plate tops, some clear anodized and some black anodized. Drawings and diagrams are mounted to the plates and etched into the aluminum. Two finished plywood plates extend beyond the table edge to form the site surface of a large, detailed model. The exhibit was presented in association with the exhibition *Aluminum by Design: Jewelry to Jets*, which ran from November 2000 through February 2001.

1.20   Ten Decades

In recognition of Rice University School of Architecture's centennial in 2012, a graphic time line was constructed of the school's history, reflecting the transition of Rice Architecture's curriculum and culture from the Beaux-Arts traditions of early twentieth-century architectural education, through the influences of modernism and advances in material and information technologies, to the contemporary global context.

   This rich, multifaceted history is depicted through ten interactive accordion books, each representing one decade from 1912 to 2012. The books serve as comparative time lines that organize information about the emerging school of architecture — its people, operations, engagement, space, outreach, and initiatives — in relation to local, national, and international influences, whether architectural, institutional, or technological. Information types are distinguished by vivid colors, highlighting the density of influences or individuals within and between decades.

1.21   First Architecture Biennale Rotterdam (1ab)

80   Information—Shape

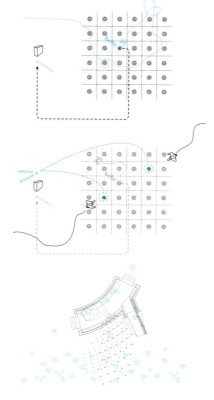

We were one of eight international architecture offices invited to design a *stim*, or site-specific interactive installation, whether an object, image, or space, that creates a moment of connectivity and intense engagement.

     Our experimental proposal, Log, uses simple digital technologies to create a spatial dynamic where fixed material elements become balanced with the real-time circumstances of pedestrian intrigue and engagement. Hard and soft systems coordinate and fuse for a brief duration, then disappear, making visible and experiential the basic infrastructures and technologies that underlie everyday urban experiences.

1.22   If-Then Mat

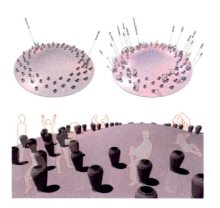

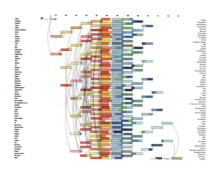

An alternate proposal for 1ab was the If-Then Mat. As with all of our proposals for the biennale, familiarly scaled architectural components used information and technology to elicit public engagement in an urban context.

     Arrayed in concentric rings on a rubber-coated circular mat are thirty-two cast aluminum toggles, each twenty-four inches high. At the top of each toggle a rubber-coated, spring-activated sensor is mounted within an illuminated ring. Pressing the soft rubber face activates the sensor. At the base, a pliable joint allows each toggle to deflect slightly when weight is applied laterally. Each is wired to a central server where signals sent from the sensor in one toggle are sorted and sent to two or more toggles at other points along the concentric rings. Each of the toggles is tagged with one of thirty-two languages and one of sixty-four prerecorded voice signals stored in the central server—"hello" and "goodbye."

1.23   Do Post

Notes No. 1

Dawn Finley was commissioned by the Dutch design consortium Droog to design and fabricate a mailbox for Do Create, a product design collection presented at the Milan Furniture Fair 2000. Each product in the collection required the consumer to complete or activate the product by interacting with it. Do Post modifies the familiar residential mailbox to allow for two-way conversations between strangers. When users post a letter, another letter is automatically delivered to them, posted by a previous user. A simple pivot and spring mechanism within the postbox stores the newly posted letter while releasing a stored letter. This is the only postbox with instant response. It can be used to register a complaint, write a secret, or post a shopping list. At a moment when digital exchanges were beginning to dominate the communication landscape, Do Post reasserted the value of the simple analog note passed between strangers. The object maintains its given type and shape (it is still recognizable as a mailbox) but reimagines the types of interaction and exchange such an object can facilitate.

1.24   Mailbox

An early prototype of Do Post was produced for an arboretum in Ann Arbor, Michigan. A grove of trees near a prominent university was chosen as the site for the curious object of exchange. Strapped to a tree using simple cables, this vernacular take on the mailbox (which calls to mind the ubiquitous sap cans found on trees in northern states during syrup-harvesting season) contains in its interior a delicate copper pivot mechanism, visible through a pane of glass, that will deliver an (also visible) envelope and the (scandalous/ funny/romantic/generous) anonymous message waiting to be read inside.

1.25   Road Sign Remix

Each year thousands of road signs are discarded due to damage caused by roadside accidents or weathering. More are decommissioned due to roadway changes and upgrades. Road signs are composite panels made of UV-resistant laminate material adhered to 0.125-inch aluminum sheets. They are generally not recyclable, as the laminate material cannot be easily removed from the aluminum. Artists in the late twentieth century sourced iconic sign material for its cultural references and graphic impact. Rosalie Gascoigne, for example, produced minimalist cut-and-paste composites, dematerializing painted wood signs to their graphic surface, while Boris Bally used the aluminum substrate to brake-form furniture and household goods. These works inspired Open Transfer's bold rainscreen panel application—reimagining the material and graphic value of the discarded signs while referencing the postwar American city's pervasive automobile culture.

1.26   Urbanism

82   Information—Shape

To understand the shape and extent of an urban space is to understand the periodicity of systems at work. In Houston in the late 1990s, old urbanism had not become *new urbanism*; it had become wholly distributed. Movement, event, mapping, deployment, and spectacle acquired new meaning and value for U.S. cities like Houston—more so than the pattern-making or collages of the traditional urban centers of the coasts.

1.27   Knockout

In graphic design, the term *knockout* refers to a shape or figure removed from a two-dimensional graphic surface (whether a pattern, image, or color field) to reveal another graphic behind. The visual effect introduces depth to a secondary space beyond the original two-dimensional surface. The knockout optically balances the negotiation of the two-dimensional surface with three-dimensional effects. Open Transfer seeks a spatial, architectural equivalent (or conceptual translation) to the knockout in graphic design through two distinct and simultaneous experiences. When viewed from outside the platform, the canopy appears as a bold, graphic icon, vibrant in color and form, with an almost monumental tone. When viewed from the platform, or from an approaching vehicle on Main Street, the color and form recede. The white undersurface brackets and frames the background of the city, highlighting a second experience and understanding of the transfer station.

The acclaimed twentieth-century graphic designer Paul Rand deployed the knockout technique to humorous and communicative effect, as shown in his 1968 poster design for Aiga and 1970 annual report cover for Westinghouse.

1.28   Press

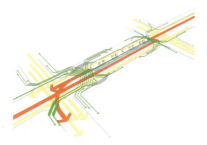

The Central Station Main Competition, organized by Houston METRO, Houston Rapid Transit, and the Houston Downtown Management District, received national attention and heightened public awareness about the value of public transportation, city infrastructure, and design. Invited architects included Interloop—Architecture, Neil M. Denari Architects, Snøhetta, LTL Architects, and SHoP Architects. The competition also generated a political divide and did not achieve the full support of local agencies and constituents. Unfortunately, a winning proposal was never publicly announced.

1.29   Fidelity of Shape

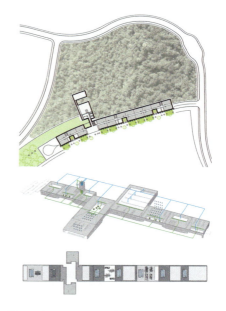

Open Transfer uses a familiar, trusted three-dimensional shape, one that is repeated throughout our work: the long bar with asymmetrical extensions, aka the "snake that swallowed a squirrel." We have tested the fidelity of the shape at various scales, materials, programs, and sites, including an exhibition display table for the Houston Products Lab, an institutional building for the Hempstead Research Center, and a sixty-unit housing project for Howard Hughes Medical Institute. The use of familiar figures and shapes is intentionally consistent throughout our work. We diligently shepherd a familiar, endearing shape from project to project, confident that novelty emerges from the unique influences of its systemic context and material assembly.

Part 2

Procedure— Assembly

Procedure—Assembly

92	48' House
106	Klip
118	E-X-I-T
134	Tending,(blue)
148	Notes No. 2

In architecture, the term *assembly* is typically understood within a manufacturing context, as the bringing together of material components, parts, and pieces to create a physical structure, detail, or building increment. Architects principally engage in assembly as practice, navigating and coordinating disparate, standard, and custom material systems in the production/formation of buildings and sites. As such, assembly is an essential disciplinary procedure and skill, not to mention a notable act of creative, selective synthesis.

The legal and contractual formats employed by architects, including construction and specifications documents, manage and define precise relationships between materials, fabrication, and manufacturers. Our professional experiences and engagement with the processes that influence architectural outcomes, however, foreground the term *assembly* to include the gathering of services, expertise, capital, protocols, tools, techniques, participants, advocacy, information, materials, and so on. In other words, the procedural aspects of each architectural project are equally important and necessarily require inclusion in the criteria that ultimately shape architecture (or design more broadly). This definition of *assembly* elevates the operative contingencies and physical constraints that precede, coincide with, and follow each project, acknowledging their impact on design methods, opportunities for innovation, and outcomes. In our office, we examine and organize these diverse elements to better understand where architectural agency can most productively be located in each project. Of course, design contingencies and opportunities vary from project to project, with each one demanding a new act of assembly. Our approach to architectural practice thus constitutes a substantive, arguably necessary, act of design—opening avenues for innovation through explicit engagement with procedures.

The assembly and organization of architectural participants is hardly new. The internal analysis and organizational methods that emerged within global architecture practices after World War II valued the principles of assembly primarily for what they contributed to the management of the complexity of large-scale international projects. Modeled after the illustrations used in scientific research, diagrams and graphic depictions of the various participants mainly identified managerial hierarchies and appropriate lines of communication (see note 2.30). Protocols and procedures were relatively fixed within divisions of architectural labor and were not regarded within a broader scope of creative contingency.

Today, advances in communication, manufacturing, and material technologies have led to protocols for architectural practice that are more open, fluid, and complex. Contemporary relationships between the design, fabrication, and implementation of buildings are far more pliable. Our work explicitly engages this context, claiming and inserting new procedures to reshape design practice in compelling and provocative ways through built and speculative work.

The following four projects—48' House (a residence and workshop), Klip (a housing delivery system), E-X-I-T (an emergency life-safety fixture), and Tending,(blue) (a building to house a commissioned artwork)—demonstrate distinct, diverse circumstances of procedure and assembly in design. Two projects question issues of housing in the United States, the first working within the given system of material trade protocols for a single-family house, and the second sidestepping home mortgage conventions to introduce a service-based housing platform. Two additional projects navigate lighting technologies, specialty engineering, manufacturing, and regulatory constraints, the first in the design of a specialized life-safety lighting product, and the second in the design of a tiny building with complex performance requirements (it must both house and function as an artwork).

48' House

48' House is a single-family residence and workspace located in Houston. Built in 2006, just before the U.S. housing crisis, the small size of the house was considered a liability by banks and lenders during a housing bubble that sought to maximize residential lots in Houston's inner loop. In return for building minimally, we (the clients) were penalized with a high interest rate. Just a few short years following the housing crisis, "building small" became an envi-ronmental, economic, and lifestyle trend in the United States—one that banks took note of as they were reforming their lending practices and procedures in the wake of the financial crisis.

Our modest design works within the conventions and constraints of residential construction practices in the United States, using a strict four-by-eight-foot framing module that resulted in fewer material cuts on-site and minimal material waste during construction. Our office deliberately eliminated de-tail drawings from the construction documents, instead noting "verify-in-field" for specific areas in the design that required coordination between off-the-shelf material components and standard residential construction details. This notation prompted on-site discussion, coordination, and detail development among the architect, contractor, and various building professionals.

The tectonic simplicity and financial economy of the house later inspired the launch of Hometta, an innovative web-based design delivery service cofounded by our office with a developer and select group of architects. Hometta worked within slightly modified modes of architecture practice to align with market-driven building production (i.e., it shortcuts but works within the sys-tem). It featured construction documents—plan, section, and elevation drawings—for contemporary houses under 2,500 square feet, designed by American architects. Hometta was the first subscription-based, open-source, house design system to allow architects and designers direct participation in the housing industry (see note 2.01).

Klip

The next project circumvents the limits of residential construction in an effort to propose a more expansive future for how we imagine, construct, and ac-quire housing. Klip is a consumer-based housing platform, an experimental delivery service that provides the physical and operational infrastructure for trade corporations to participate in the production of high-performance residential components. The system was developed for Sixteen Houses, a competition and public exhibition project organized in 1998 by the architect Michael Bell with support from the Graham Foundation and DiverseWorks in Houston. We were one of sixteen design offices invited to generate innovative concepts for a low-income house. The project's aim was to expand the limited options available to those individuals who qualified for federal and state housing vouchers. Vouchers guaranteed financial assistance for select families and individuals, enabling them to make the necessary down payment on the purchase of a house. In its current form, the voucher system distributes a mass of capital such that one voucher equals one house.

Our office was frustrated with residential design systems that are constricted by insurance companies, loan officers, municipalities, and contractors—an assembly that often exerts greater influence on the design of buildings and cities than do architects. We calculated the overall economic impact that these vouchers might have if, rather than being distributed to individual families, they were to allow investment in new housing opportunities. We researched consumer products and services, from automobiles to appliances to computers, along with the payment and finance structures, performance expectations, warranties, customizations, and upgrades available for each. We began to imagine how these benefits could be applied to the acquisition and maintenance of a house. Our Klip concept consolidated the vouchers to pay for a housing platform; that is, both a housing infrastructure and a system of services. We had to work outside the home mortgage process to gain ground. Klip was motivated by the competition brief and public exhibition, which allowed for more extreme speculation and innovation.

Innovation, like other impulses in the design field, is regulated. Professional institutions created to support architecture often undermine proposals for unprecedented structures, components, and elements. Most contractual language associated with the construction industry deliberately avoids risk, a fundamental characteristic of innovation. However, some design circumstances justify the crossing of disciplinary lines and the extension of the procedural limits of architectural practice to engage the complexities and inherent liabilities of other industries. By doing so in the case of Klip, we recaptured some of the innovative sensibility apparently written out of our discipline by insurance policies, professional associations, and regulatory agencies.

E-X-I-T

Projects often emerge in unexpected ways and sometimes redirect our disciplinary attention to new formats. Like many architects, we specify numerous fixtures for the buildings we design, whether they be lighting, hardware, furniture, or life-safety components. During the specification process for one client in the early 2000s, we were asked to research the market availability of alternative life-safety exit-light fixtures. To our surprise, advances in exit-light design have been incredibly limited, falling broadly into two basic formal categories: fixtures with a solid background contrasting the four letters (E-X-I-T) and optional chevron; and edge-lit, glass-plate fixtures that attempt to minimize the boxy appearance of the sign. While many twentieth-century architects have received accolades for limited edition light-fixture designs, our research revealed that no architect had designed a life-safety exit-light fixture, nor were there any

Procedure—Assembly

formal alternatives to the two basic categories. Our interest in and research of the systems that regulate exit lights continued far beyond this initial client. Had we known at the time what we know now about the challenges of proposing and manufacturing what we refer to as "free-floating letters," a seemingly modest aesthetic improvement to what is on the market, we might never have begun work on the first custom exit light in the United States designed by architects.

E-X-I-T is a life-safety emergency light fixture designed and manufactured by our office in collaboration with a range of material suppliers, engineers, and fabricators. In keeping with city, state, and federal safety standards, every emergency light fixture must undergo extensive examination, testing, and approval by various agencies, with little concern for innovation. The project prompted us to make broad connections between fabrication processes, lighting technologies, industrial design, and legislative safety standards overseen and implemented by Underwriter Laboratories (UL). Our considerable research on the production and distribution of life-safety fixtures in the United States revealed that few resources exist to help navigate the complex procedures required for innovation in this area.

We engaged directly with UL agents, quickly became experts in light-emitting diode technologies, and developed new sensibilities toward the UL technical requirements. Then, rather than work with traditional lighting fabricators and suppliers, we outsourced the fabrication of material and electronic components to a diverse range of Houston-based companies that typically serve the petroleum, medical, and aerospace industries. Rather than allow the processes surrounding the production and deployment of emergency lighting systems to dictate and ultimately eliminate opportunities for invention, we assumed the role of the industry specialist and redirected the efforts of local companies with the capacity, if not yet the expertise, to produce exit-light fixtures. One of our original prototype exit-light fixtures was inducted into the permanent collection of the Museum of Modern Art (MoMA) in 2007, marking a departure in MoMA's collecting policy and providing an early precedent for the inclusion of architectural signage artifacts.

Tending,(blue)   In 2002, we were commissioned by the Nasher Foundation to design a museum-quality building to house *Tending,(blue)*, an artwork by the internationally acclaimed artist James Turrell. The open-air building is sited in a planted berm at one end of a lush garden across from the main museum building in Dallas. The full project and site assembles an array of client participants, curators, artists, and state and city agencies, a high-profile design architect (Renzo Piano Building Workshop, RPBW), and a well-known landscape architect (Peter Walker and Partners, PWP).

While the free-standing building was subject to strict national and local building codes, the operative and aesthetic performance criteria mandated by the artist's commission, coupled with the geothermal ambitions of the building's siting in the garden, amplified the complexity of the project's material and technological integration. Our role in design, quite simply, was to coordinate and synthesize material, light, temperature, and sound, in both time and space.

The precise interaction of light, space, and dynamic human visual perception is critical to each of Turrell's artworks. While the architecture establishes the ideal environmental conditions essential to experiencing one of his works, it is often considered secondary, a background to the visual encounter. That is, because it participates in generating and enabling the artwork's striking optical effects, the architecture is neither formally nor materially neutral—yet it is expected to modestly recede in deference to the artwork.

The project represents a significant departure in the technical systems and light sources used for a Turrell skyspace and also includes highly specialized building services for the year-round open-air structures. Our office surveyed a wide range of topics and technologies for the diverse technical requirements of the building. Some of these related to the performance of the artwork (e.g., theatrical lighting systems and special effects, LED and cold cathode lighting, lunar and solar calendars, concealed mechanical systems), and others were a consequence of the climate and site (e.g., water coil systems for heated seats, air flow, drainage, and water collection). Once we had determined the technical requirements, our office transitioned to the design of new assemblies for these complex interacting systems and sequences. We were responsible for learning the software interface and all commands, getting various technology platforms to communicate, engineering complex scheduling techniques to synchronize solar and computational clocks, running mixing boards, and interpreting the artist's intended effects. Lighting, dimming, and recording systems, and full-size mock-ups were used to test the component combinations relative to brightness, control, and color resolution. Ultimately, the new light source and dimming system allowed for the programming of variable lighting settings, tuned to produce specific visual effects in relation to the solar conditions of downtown Dallas. Effects were programmed to change daily and seasonally, allowing the artwork to produce a greater range of experiences.

Our approach to assembly, which includes the operative procedures of design, neither negates nor depreciates the value of physical, material connections at the scale of buildings and details in architecture. Rather, the methods of professional engagement (or that allow and facilitate practice) are fundamental and cannot be disentangled from the making of architecture.

48' House

Client   Finley & Wamble
Dates   2004–2006
Location   Houston, Texas

Built in 2006, just before the U.S. housing crisis, the small size of the house was considered a liability by banks and lenders during a housing bubble that sought to maximize residential lots in Houston's inner loop.

The 48' House is a single-family residence and workspace. Located in Houston, it was designed for both our architectural practice and our family. The ground floor contains a generous office space and an open carport that also serves as an outdoor room for entertaining. The second level is the primary living space, organized by a forty-eight-foot-long room that accommodates dining, living, and lounging to the north, with a kitchen, stair, and private bedrooms to the south. Combined with large windows on the north and south facades, this elevated arrangement simultaneously allows for privacy from the street and views through the tree canopies into the front yard and the neighboring community. Designed to minimize the building footprint and maximize outdoor spaces for gardening and recreation, the house is a compact 1,800 square feet. The aim of the 48' House was a more modestly scaled domestic life, and the house was featured nationally in the October 2007 "New American Home" issue of *Dwell* for its economy and restraint.

While the property's setback restriction mandates a minimum of twenty-five feet, the house is resolutely sited seventy-five feet from the street at the far end of a lot that backs up to Interstate 59. Enclosing the narrow backyard is a sound wall beyond which runs the highway, eighteen feet below natural grade. From the second level of the house, oak tree–canopied residential areas and the high rises of the Texas Medical Center are visible to the south. The open carport works spatially and mechanically with the adjacent houses to the east and west, whose forward siting (in accordance with the twenty-five-foot setback) produces a plenum-like condition that draws a steady flow of air from the freeway to the open lawn at the north side of the property. The mass of the house blocks the majority of traffic sounds, making the front lawn ideal for outdoor family activities.

The house design is based on a strict four-by-eight-foot framing module, both in plan and elevation, which is ideal for standard wood systems and creates minimal material waste during construction. The design's economy and simplicity allowed for a few custom architectural pieces, including a powder-coated perforated steel guardrail; a set of tall, perforated steel laundry doors; and a painted wood credenza.

48' House

Assembly
list

Site, Client, Loan Officer, Demolition Crew, Architect, Deed Restrictions, Survey, Construction Loan, Structural Engineer, Geotechnical Engineer, Construction Documents, Expediter, Building Permits, General Contractor, Concrete Installers, Structural Inspections, Framers, Plumbers, Electricians, Mechanical Subcontractor, Building Inspections, Loan Inspections, Painters, Specialty Fabricator, Ikea, Best Buy, Amazon, Landscape Consultant, Certificate of Occupancy, Photographer, Writer, Publisher

96 Procedure—Assembly

The site backs up to a fourteen-foot-high masonry sound wall adjacent to a deep zone of planting (eucalyptus, cypress, and oak trees, and a variety of flowering plant species) that buffers US Interstate 59. The sound wall is not visible through the lush plantings.

48' House

Procedure—Assembly

Interior and exterior views

Dining and living area with custom perforated guardrail and laundry doors.

2" x 6" tongue-and-groove pine decking serves as the floor structure and finish.

100   Procedure—Assembly

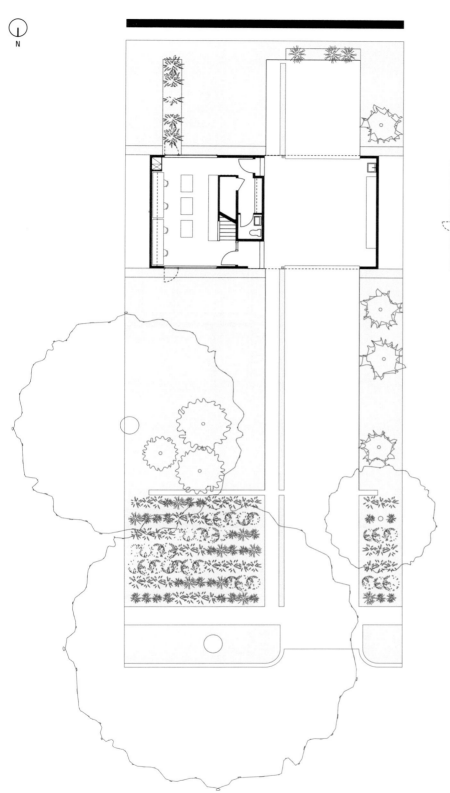
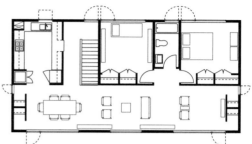

Ground floor workspaces: covered shop, office, storage, and half bath.

Second floor living spaces: kitchen, dining, lounge area, bedrooms, and full bath.

48' House

Sections

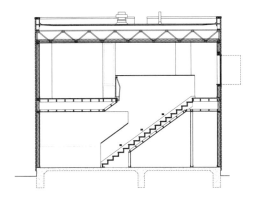
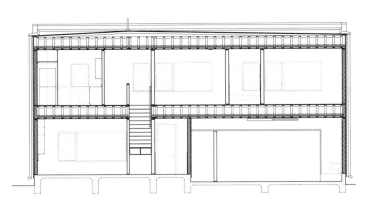
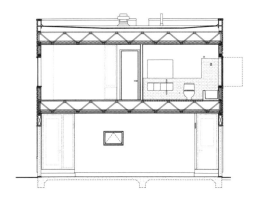
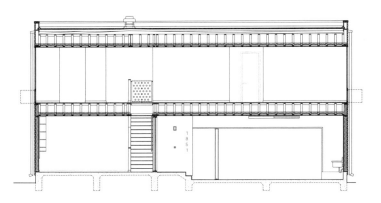

Procedure—Assembly

Elevations

Repetitive window sizes
require a measured composition
of the building elevations.

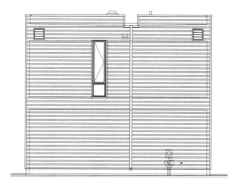
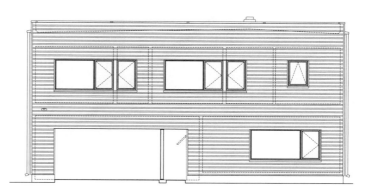
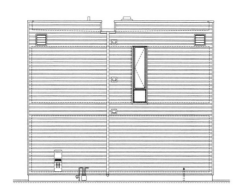
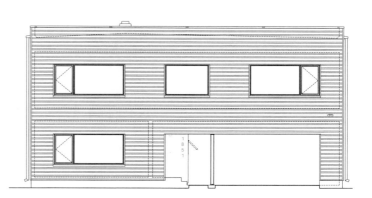

48' House

Previous page: Detail at operable windows, view through dining area, and activity in the front lawn

This page: Workspace with built-in cabinets for books, models, and material samples

Klip

Client	Fifth Ward Community Redevelopment Corporation & DiverseWorks
Dates	1998
Location	Houston, Texas

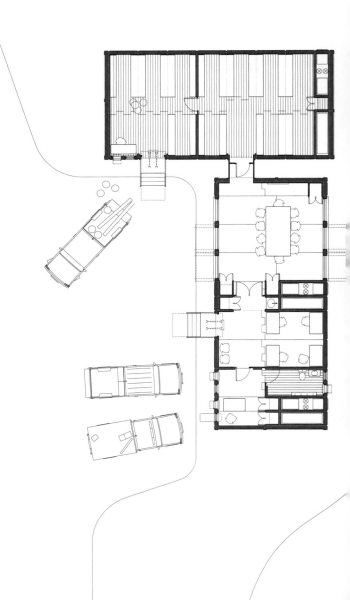

Klip is a consumer-based housing platform, an experimental delivery service that provides the physical and operational infrastructure for trade corporations to produce *advanced living* components. These additive, reconfigurable components are designed to meet a diverse range of contemporary lifestyles based on service as the primary housing commodity. As the mock advertisements we created for the project explain, "Just as you might upgrade your TV or trade in your automobile, the Klip system responds to your changing housing needs. 24-hour service, on-line trade-in options, money-back guarantee, buy one get one free, all major credit cards accepted."

Klip was developed during our participation in Sixteen Houses, a competition and public exhibition project organized and curated in 1998 by the architect and academic Michael Bell and funded by the Graham Foundation, the Fifth Ward Community Redevelopment Corporation, and DiverseWorks in Houston. Sixteen architects and designers from across the United States were invited to generate innovative options for a low-income

106   Procedure—Assembly

Our office was frustrated with residential design systems that are constricted by insurance companies, loan officers, municipalities, and contractors— an assembly that often exerts greater influence on the design of buildings and cities than do architects.

house, the aim being to expand the limited marketplace available for those with access to emerging federal and state voucher programs that provide financial assistance (i.e., for a down payment on a house purchase) to qualified families and individuals. In its current form, the voucher system does not allow vouchers to be combined—one voucher thus provides enough capital for only one house. Reluctant to design a single house that had little impact on the housing industry, our concept consolidated the vouchers to pay for a housing platform or infrastructure.

Klip assembles fabricators, distributors, and a wide range of specialized expertise to participate and produce high-performance housing components. These components are available in three- and six-foot widths, each available with a variety of product, fixture, and service options. Mass-produced pieces of binding equipment serve as the housing infrastructure. Binders are deployed between an open array of components that can be added, released, interchanged, upgraded, and rearranged through customized and cataloged

configurations. (In skiing and snowboarding, the binder is the most critical piece of high-performance equipment, as it attaches the body to the board and effectively to the ground. We took this notion as a point of development, creating an adjustable footing system for housing components.)

In presenting the proposal, we considered the aftermarket material consequences of a housing platform, anticipating its future disassembly and redistribution, and subsequent reuse of parts. "All components are take-home and Klip compatible," our mock advertisements noted. "Maintenance, exchange, upgrades and return services are provided through your local Klip dealer, or by way of the usual home shopping outlets. Your satisfaction is guaranteed." We speculated that production material types would be limited for ease of identification and sorting in years to come. Dealerships were anticipated as a secondary, specialized trade to recondition and resell used platform components.

Assembly list

Fifth Ward Community Redevelopment Corporation, DiverseWorks, Graham Foundation, Sixteen Architects, Federal and State Housing Vouchers, City of Houston, High-Performance Binding Equipment, Corporate Participants, Order Forms, Fabricators, Housing Modules, Catalogs, Dealerships, Leasing and Purchasing Options, Warranties, Maintenance and Service Contracts, Trade-In Policies, Upgrades, Advertising, Aftermarket Parts, Recycling

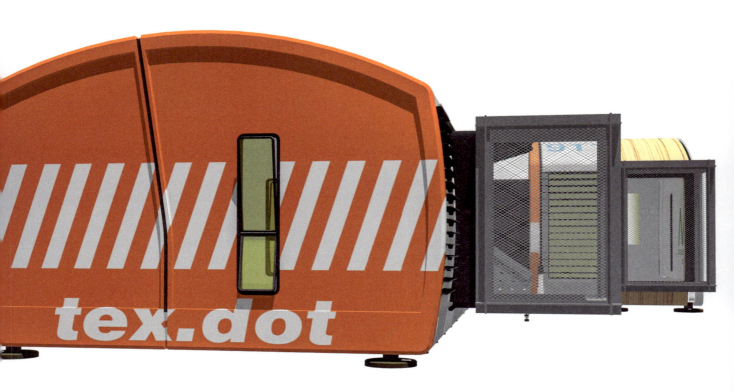

Ramping Up: Klip and Component Partners — New Products: Klip and Component Partners

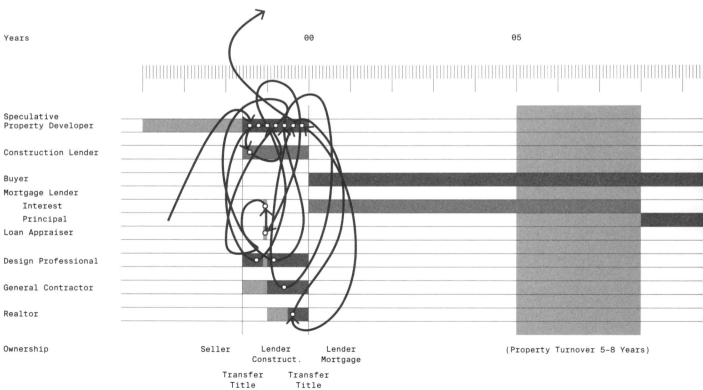

110   Procedure—Assembly

New Products: Klip and Component Partners

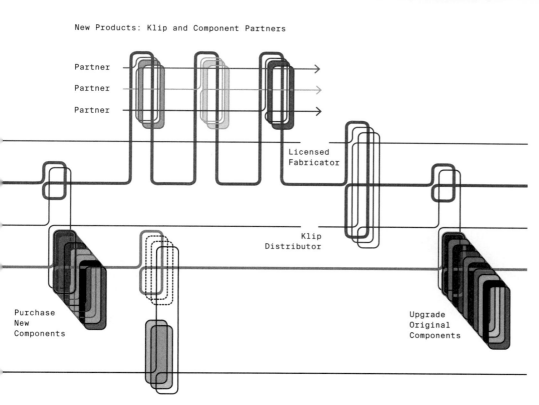

Service diagram speculates how a service-based housing system might work. Equity can be built incrementally; building along the way rather than all at once reduces risk. Klip is essentially engaging financing systems that exist in the automotive and home appliance industries. Power structures, in economic terms, are redistributed to enable private investment in housing at a manageable scale. Innovation for Klip is that it is service-based rather than product-based.

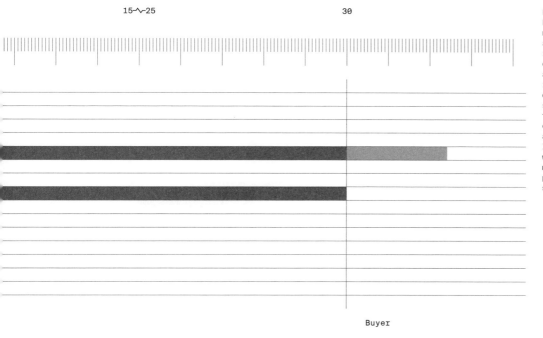

Product diagram describes how a standard thirty-year mortgage loan works. Federal and state housing-voucher initiatives that give opportunities using vouchers as a down payment (while well intended) still make use of the mortgage system—one significant financial strain for a low-income household could be enough to cause a family to default on their loan, losing everything. Klip works outside of the home mortgage process, providing a platform for delivering and servicing the house.

Klip

Platform

Components are available in three- and six-foot widths, each made available with a variety of options. With the Klip delivery system, components are either bought or leased.

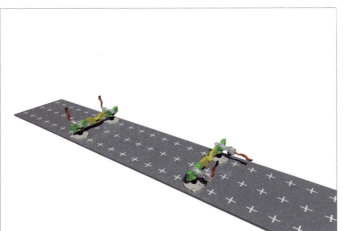

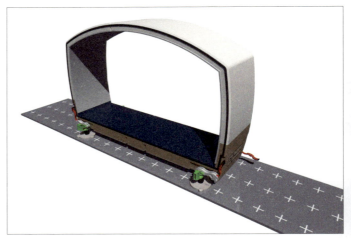

Four binders with adjustable footings support two six-foot-wide interlocking components.

112   Procedure—Assembly

Binder

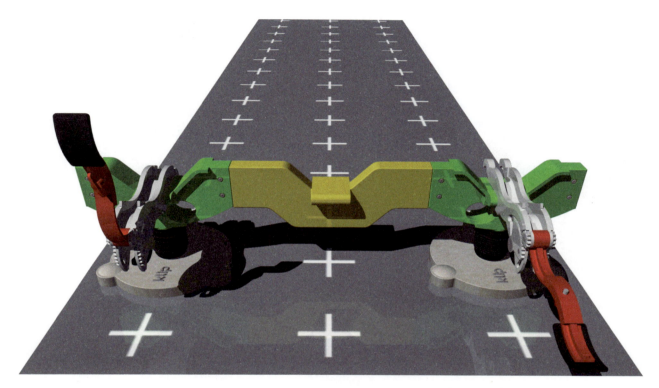

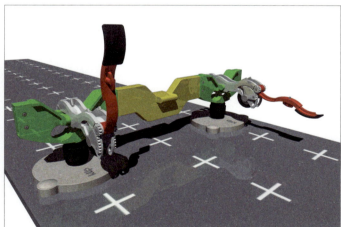
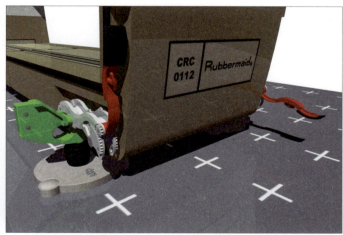

Two binders with adjustable footings and rail shown in the locked and unlocked positions, then fit with a six-foot-wide Rubbermaid manufactured component.

Klip

These images take into account an extreme material consequence of aftermarket used and refurbished components.

114   Procedure—Assembly

Order Form: House configurations are assembled from a catalog of components and binders that can be leased or purchased from local authorized dealerships.

www.kliphouse.com

DATE	01 / 27 / 01
INVOICE NO.	0000728
TRANSACTION NO.	#000141
EMPLOYEE	Martin 0006

CUSTOMER INFORMATION

Property Mates
456 Bristol Lane
Houston, TX 77006-3802
(713) 527-1111

PRODUCT INFORMATION

BINDER LICENSE NO.	0000728
ASSEMBLY CONFIGURATION	Double Rail
UTILITY CODE	3
VOUCHER NO.	US 89786348-9454-77226TX

ITEM NO.	BRAND / COMPONENT	SIZE.	QTY.	TYPE	SPEC.
6651-3 bf	BFI	recycle-clip	6' x 9'	1	leased	bfi blue
0762-4 at	Atlas	utility toilet	3' x 12'	1	leased	beige
2714-3 kr	Kohler	lightShower	3' x 12'	1	leased	salmon
0394-2 ig	Igloo	snackChiller	3' x 9'	1	leased	
2475-4 rm	Rubbermaid	wetport plus	6' x 12'	1	leased	extension req.
0075-4 rm	Rubbermaid	light-extension	6' x 6'	1	leased	port req.
0977-4 ml	Maglite	stripklip	3' x 9'	1	leased	fluorescent
0779-1 cc	Coca-Cola	fizzklip	3' x 9' +18"	1	leased	service
0098-7 dh/fa	DieHard/Frigidaire	power/aircool	3' x 12'	1	leased	service
2369-1 oz/wh	Ozarka/Whirlpool	deluxeklip	6' x 12'	1	purchased	service
2278-8 co	Coleman	cookerklip	3' x 9'	1	purchased	red
0394-2 sz	SubZero	chillklip	3' x 9'	1	leased	
0633-1 mx	Maxell	zip-klip	3' x 9'	1	leased	
8956-5 rs	Radio Shack	network/power	3' x 12'	1	lease	
0716-1 lb	La-Z-boy	foldout-sleeper	6' x 9'	1	lease	
0457-2 vw/tr	VW/Trek	bike-port	3' x 12' + 24"	1	lease	car rack incl.
5933-2 ri	REI	rock-klip	3' x 12'	1	lease	
3339-6 ip	Imperial Plumbing	h2o Heater	3' x 9'	1	leased	
5566-1 ge/ar	GE/Armstrong	light-color-klip	3' x 9'	1	leased	powder blue
6430-3 bb	Best Buy	systemklip	6' x 12'	1	leased	extension req.
1189-7 dp	DuPont	connector	6' x 6'	1	leased	perp. joiner
6647-3 bf	BFI	halfport	6' x 9'	1	leased	translucent
0699-1 nk	Nike	floorgrip-klip	3' x 9'	1	purchased	
8793-1 tr	Therma-rest	singlesleep	3' x 12'	1	purchased	
0762-4 at	Atlas	filler strip	3' x 12'	1	leased	steel grey
0592-4 ps	PlaySkool	glowklip	3' x 9'	1	leased	lime fuzzy
2366-2 oz	Ozarka	h2o dispenser	3' x 9' + 24"	1	purchased	service
0098-7 dh/mx	DieHard/Maxell	battery sound	3' x 12'	1	leased	service
4386-1 ad	Adidas	sport-sleep-klip	6' x 12'	1	lease	
2475-5 co	Coleman	swingStep	6' x 9' / 6 x 12'	2	leased	SET
0098-0 wb	Weber	bar-b-klip	3' x 9'	1	leased	
1236-2 km	K-mart	greenklip	3' x 9' +24"	1	lease	
99349-1 wh	Whirlpool	toddlertubklip	3' x 12'	1	purchased	
0362-3 am	Acme	utility washerklip	3' x 12'	1	leased	beige

PRODUCT UPDATE / ANNOUNCEMENTS

Expand your house with a Playschool cradleklip #0597-2PS for that pleasant, but unexpected pregnancy.

MONTHLY TOTAL

STATE LEASE TAX

STANDARD PAYMENT

X _____
Authorized & Received By

Klip

115

Scenarios

Scenarios enable Klip to identify critical unknowns of a housing system, by isolating the routines and cycles of a house and its occupants. Represented here are three distinct use and site scenario studies for an Executive Couple, an Extended Family, and a group of Property Mates.

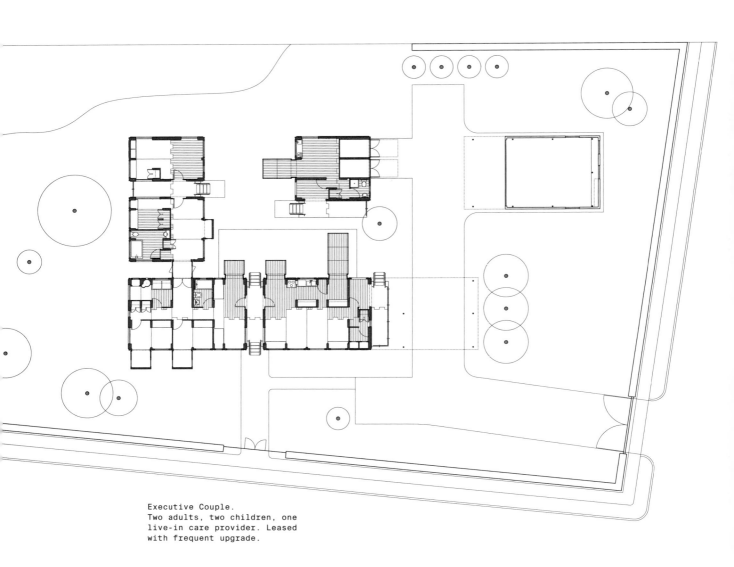

Executive Couple.
Two adults, two children, one live-in care provider. Leased with frequent upgrade.

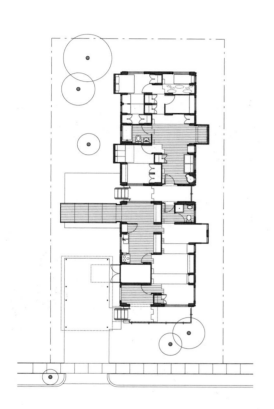

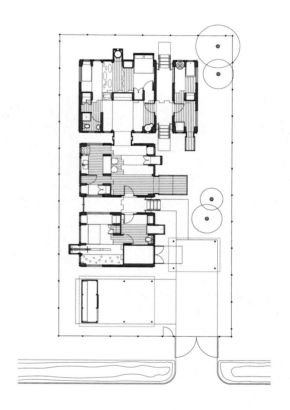

Extended Family.
Three adults, three children
(four generations). Purchased
(used) and leased components.

Property Mates.
Four single adults. Used and
reconditioned components
and binders, salvaged parts.

Klip

E-X-I-T

Client   Architectural Safety Components
Dates   2013–2019
Location Houston, Texas

118　　　　Procedure—Assembly

Rather than work with traditional lighting fabricators and suppliers, we outsourced the fabrication of material and electronic components to a diverse range of Houston-based companies that typically serve the petroleum, medical, and aerospace industries.

E-X-I-T is an award-winning life-safety emergency light fixture designed and fabricated by our office in collaboration with a range of manufacturers, suppliers, and fabricators. The fixture establishes a new set of priorities for safety-related building components, adding to its important life-safety function by incorporating aesthetic and technical ambitions into the design. The design combines a minimal graphic appearance with refined mounting options, eliminating the solid background or edge-lit glass plate that defines all other exit-light fixtures on the market. This modest yet technically challenging alteration allows the precision-cast dimensional acrylic letters and chevron to free-float from a delicate milled aluminum bracket and backplate assembly. Compact LEDs are arrayed within the dimensional legend to maximize uniformity, color, brightness, and legibility. The design and internal milling profile of the individual acrylic letters E, X, I, and T were rigorously tested (and patented) to produce an even distribution of the LED lights.

To comply with city, state, and federal safety standards, every life-safety fixture must undergo extensive testing and receive approval from various regulatory agencies. Our office thus had to make broad connections between fabrication processes, lighting technologies, industrial design, and legislative safety standards as implemented and overseen by Underwriter Laboratories.

In collaboration with an outside partner, we established an entrepreneurial start-up office, Architectural Safety Components (ASC). Production engaged through ASC is subject to market forces, impacted by trade tariffs, and localized to U.S. fabricators and suppliers, mostly in Houston. In an effort to maintain ethical labor practices, ASC does not outsource production or assembly to foreign countries.

E-X-I-T

Assembly list

Life-Safety Standards, Architects, Designers, UL Inspectors, IP Attorneys, Electrical Engineers, National Building Codes, Milling, Injection Molding, Anodizing, Powder Coating, Printed Circuit Boards, Low Voltage Wire, Battery Back-Up, Partial Assembly, Electrical Integration, UL Approval Number, Testing, On–Site Inspection, Utility Patents, Design Patent, Trademarks, Website, Lighting Distributors, Contractors, Quotes, Orders, Packaging, Installation Instructions, Delivery, Design Award, Writer, Photographer, Press

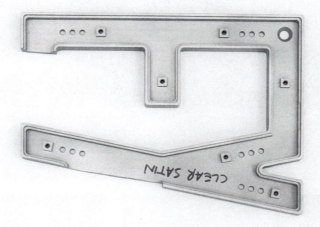

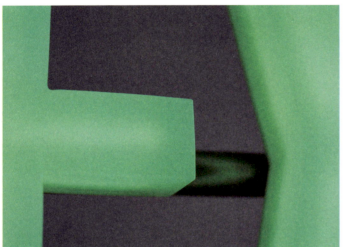
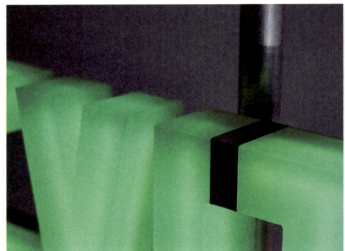

Prototypes and Design
Development Components

LELU™ fixtures use milled aluminum backplate and mounting components, while the most recent UL-approved version, ELIS™, uses snap-connected injection-molded parts.

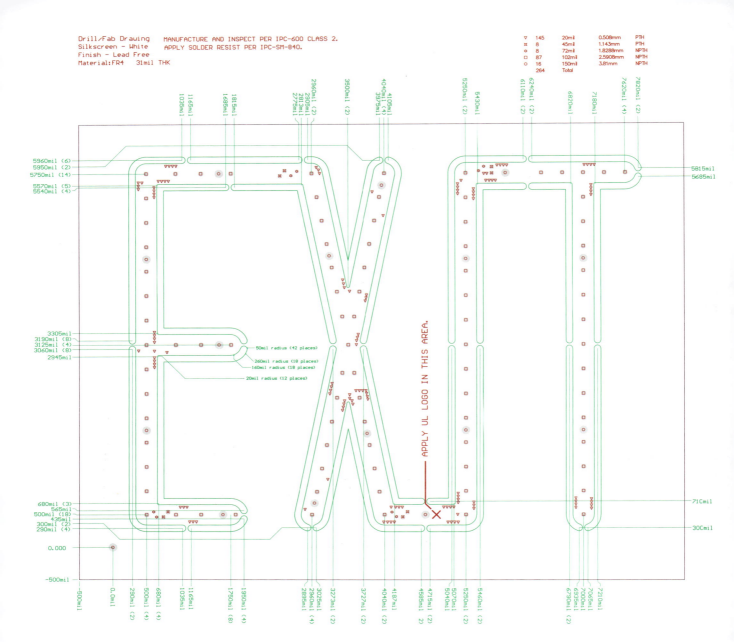

Shop drawings are vital documents
for coordinating precise material
and operational aspects of
each exit-light configuration.
We collaborate with our engineers
to develop drawings that serve
all constituents in the design,
regulatory-review, production, and
assembly processes.

124   Procedure—Assembly

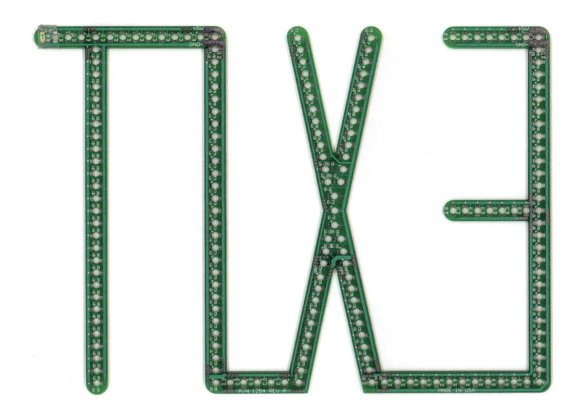

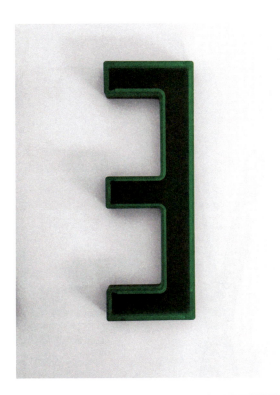

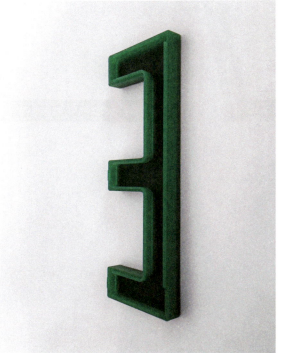

Procedure—Assembly

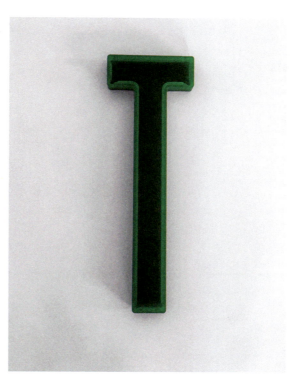

The design and internal milling
profile of the individual
acrylic letters E, X, I, and T
were rigorously tested to
produce an even distribution
of the LED lights.

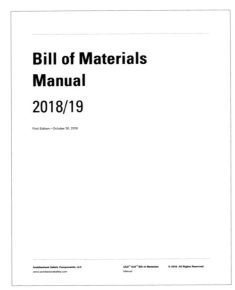
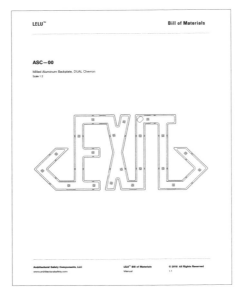
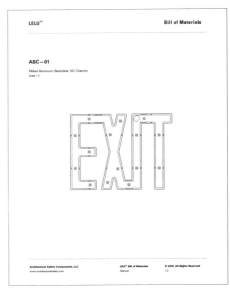

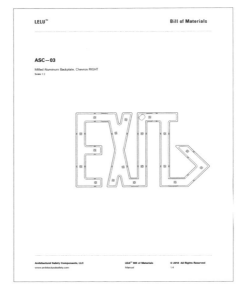
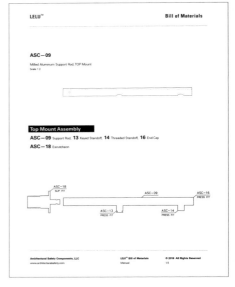
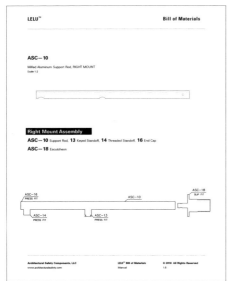
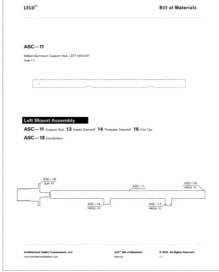
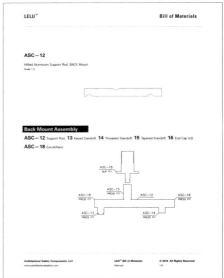

Procedure—Assembly

E-X-I-T

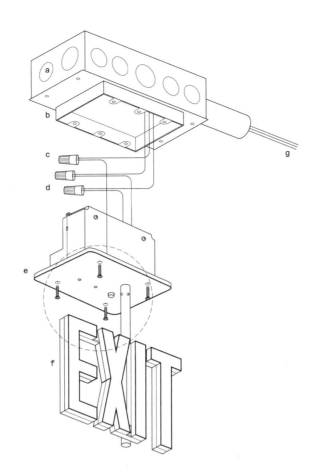

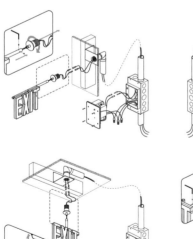
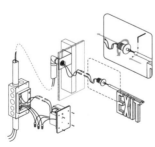
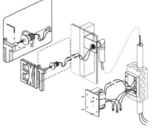

a Three-gang electrical box
b Trim ring
c Ground screw
d AC input
e Cover plate with power supply and battery
f Integral exit sign assembly
g House power and ground wire
h Battery test button
j Set screws

130   Procedure—Assembly

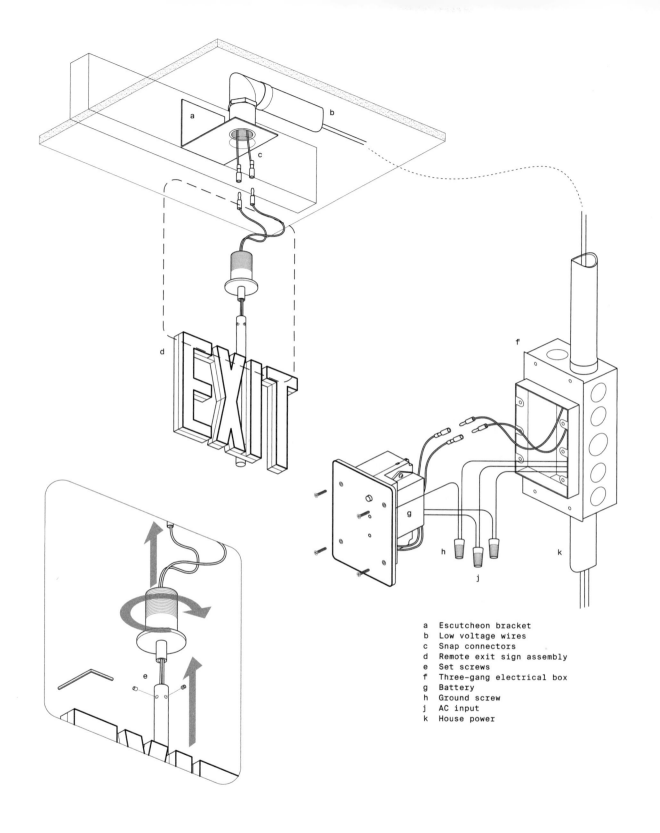

a Escutcheon bracket
b Low voltage wires
c Snap connectors
d Remote exit sign assembly
e Set screws
f Three-gang electrical box
g Battery
h Ground screw
j AC input
k House power

E-X-I-T

Remote mounting configuration locates the power source behind an aluminum face plate. The legend and tube bracket are mounted independently to a discrete, round escutcheon — allowing the exit sign to be located up to twenty feet away from the power source.

Procedure—Assembly

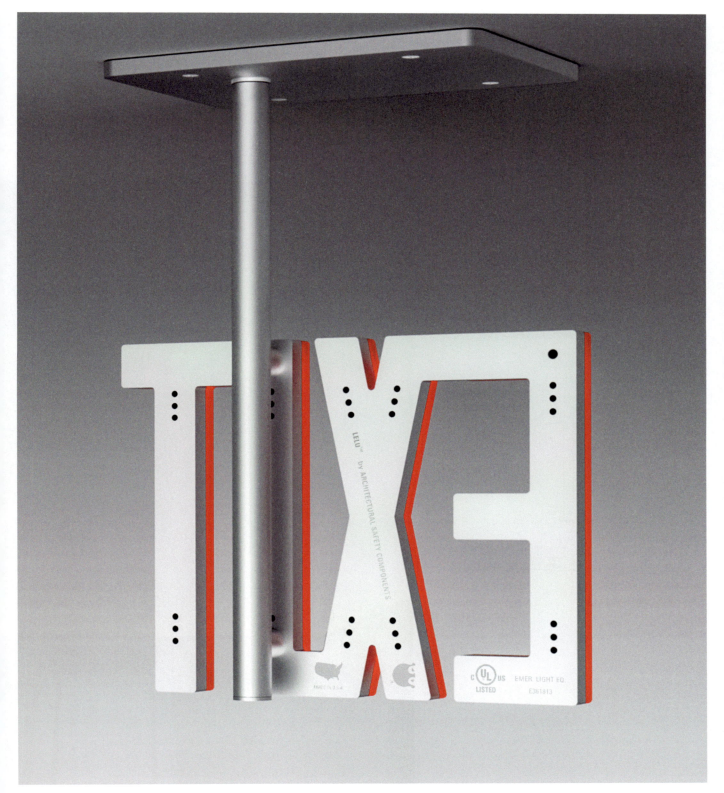

Integral mounting configuration locates the power source behind an aluminum face plate, which is attached to the surface of a wall or ceiling.

The legend and tube bracket mount directly to the face plate, giving the letters a weightless appearance.

E-X-I-T

Tending,
(blue)

Client   The Nasher Foundation
Artist   James Turrell
Dates   2001-2003
Location Dallas, Texas

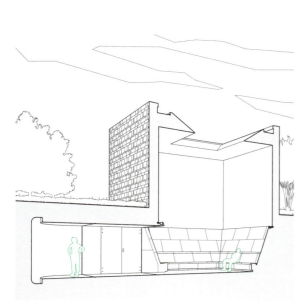

134   Procedure—Assembly

Because it participates in generating and enabling the artwork's striking optical effects, the architecture is neither formally nor materially neutral—yet it is expected to modestly recede in deference to the artwork.

We were commissioned to design a small, open-air building to house *Tending,(blue)*, a set of two artworks by the internationally acclaimed artist James Turrell. The building-artwork is nestled in a planted berm at the far end of the Nasher Sculpture Center property in downtown Dallas. The main museum building, designed by Renzo Piano Building Workshop, Genoa, is sited at the opposite end of the full city block, framing a large urban garden designed by Peter Walker and Partners and filled with one of the largest collections of modern sculpture in the world.

    Tending,(blue) contains two artworks—an entry piece and a skyspace. The modest stone entry peeks out from a lush planted berm and is visible from the garden due to its subtle, compelling blue glow. While the entry appears to lead visitors directly into the subterranean space of the berm, it creates a light-lined connection to the abstract, stacked-stone skyspace volume emerging from the top of the berm several yards away. The skyspace is a twenty-five-foot cubic space with a square nine-by-nine-foot aperture in the ceiling. This aperture is detailed as a *knife edge* to eliminate any visual perception of the roof's thickness. The four inner walls of the skyspace are lined with a continuous stone bench for seating, broken only by the entrance to the space. The top edge of the bench is above eye level, designed to conceal a collection of electrical and mechanical components required to achieve the minimal interior space. Ideal viewing of the artwork occurs during the most dramatic changes in exterior light, at dusk and dawn. The light levels on the interior are held constant, while the change in light and color in the sky is revealed through the cut in the ceiling.

Tending,(blue)

Assembly list

Client, Artist, Architect, Landscape Architect, MEP Engineers, Geotechnical Engineers, Sound Programmers, Lighting Consultants, Code Consultants, Texas Accessibility Standards (TAS), Construction Documents, Expediter, Building Permits, Local Code Officials, General Contractor, Fabricators, Installers, C.I.P. Concrete, Structural Inspection, Insulation, Stone Panels, Plaster, Dry Stack, Ductwork, Diffusers, Cold Cathodes, LEDs, Soundboard, Kinetic Armature, TAS Inspection, Landscape Installers

Tending,(blue)

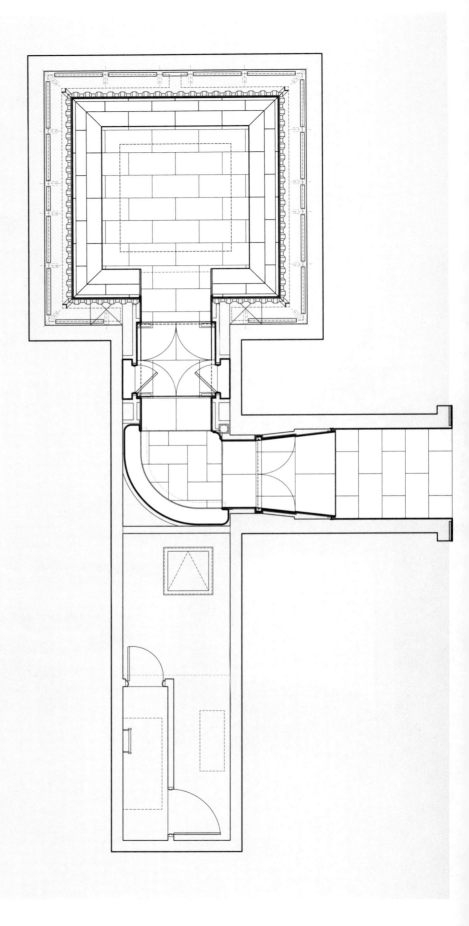

Procedure—Assembly

Previous page: Floor plan of skyspace artwork, vestibule, entrance, and mechanical room

This page: Cross section at entrance and at skyspace

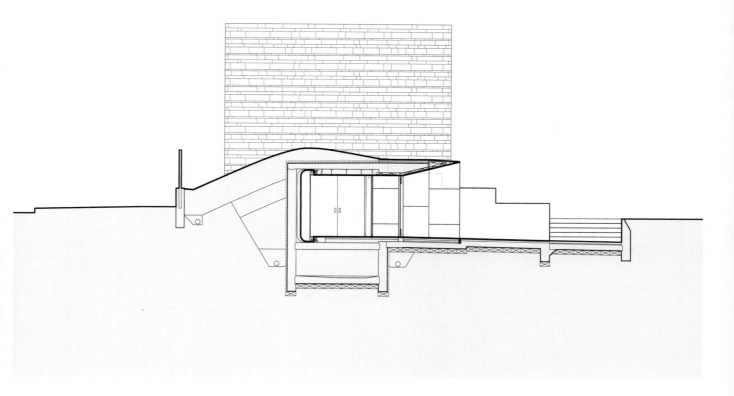

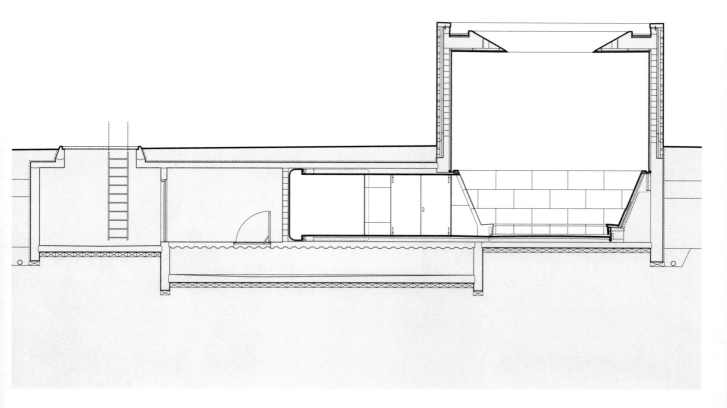

Tending,(blue)

Tending,(blue)

Lighting Program Diagrams
for Varying Environmental
Conditions

Cue #05, Program SUNRISE,
66 minutes

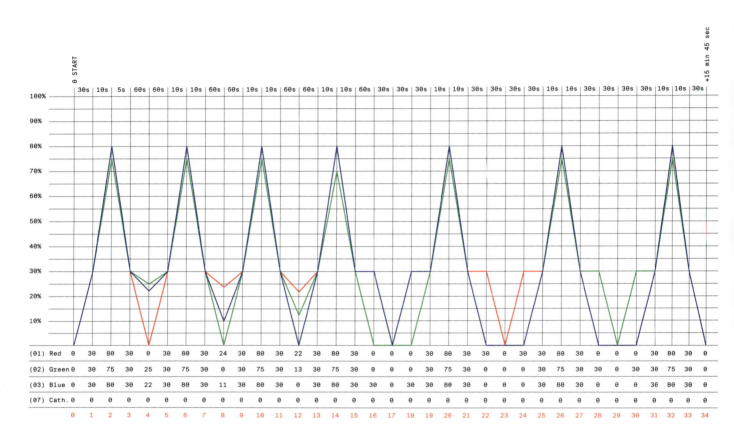

Procedure—Assembly

Cue #13, Program BLACK-OUT,
15 minutes

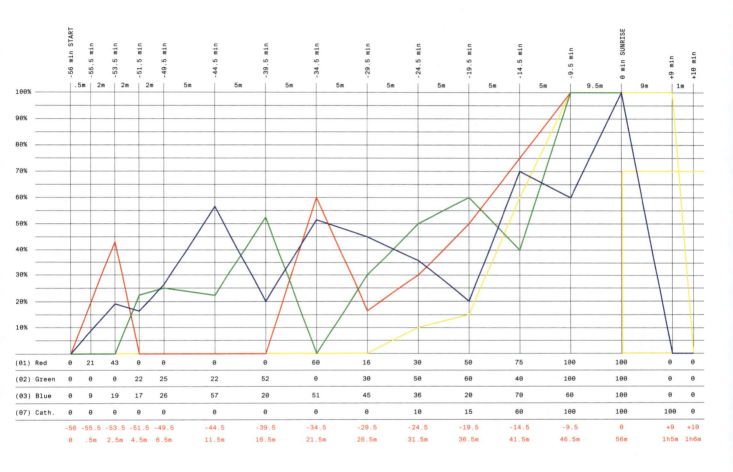

Tending,(blue)

Top: Lighting program
tests during construction
with artist James
Turrell and Mark Wamble

Aerial view of the
Nasher Sculpture Center
under construction

144   Procedure—Assembly

View from the garden walkway

Tending,(blue)

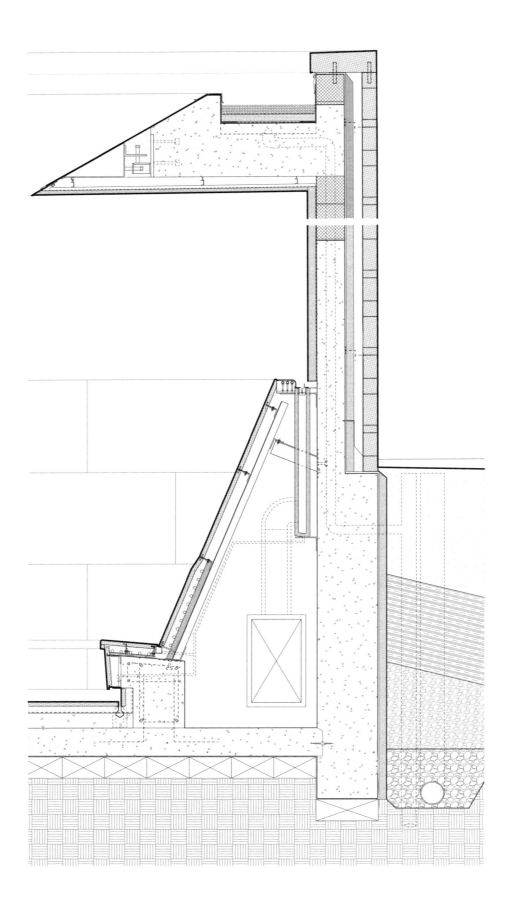

146 Procedure—Assembly

Previous page: Detailed wall section at skyspace artwork

This page: Section through mechanical/electrical room, vestibule, and skyspace; elevation from garden

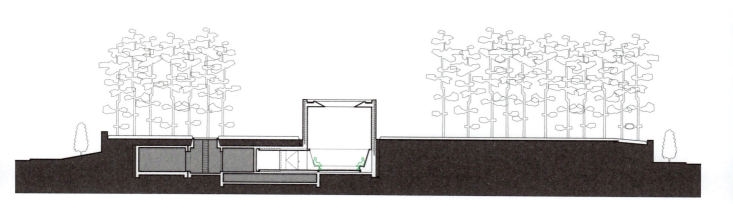

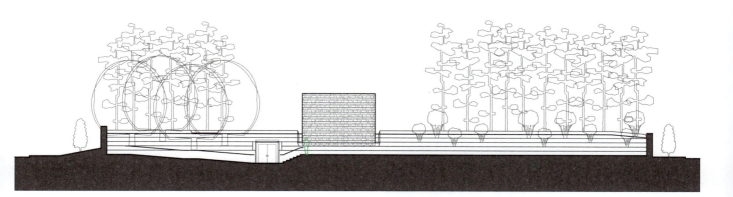

Tending,(blue) 147

Notes No. 2

Novelty may be understood as the shared experience of a new cultural circumstance or as an individual subjective perception.

2.01 Design Delivery Model

2.02 Welcome Hometta

Hometta was an innovative design delivery service—part modern home plan company, part architecture magazine, and part resource library. It was an entirely web-based set of tools that allowed prospective homeowners to engage architecture as a product, while improving the design quality of new single-family houses. Rather than try to reconceive how single-family residences are produced and delivered, Hometta modified current modes of architecture practice to align with market-driven building production. Clients purchased a set of home plans online and contracted with a local builder to construct the design.

Unlike traditional companies that offer stock building plans, Hometta partnered with progressive architects and provided resources to guide subscribers through the home-building process. The start-up received extensive national press and launched with great success. Curiously, the project resulted in more commissions for custom house designs than in actual sales of home plans. After eight years in which it built a network of collaborators and reached a broader audience of clients who were interested in design, Hometta closed its doors.

Welcome Hometta was a multicity exhibition that took place in 2009 at pinkcomma gallery in Boston, New World Gallery in Houston, and San Francisco Living Home Tours. The exhibition featured detailed, three-dimensional resin models of twenty-four home designs, assembled as a stunning neighborhood of modern houses.

2.03 Hometta, Etc.

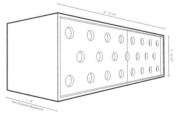

Hometta's participating architects were asked to contribute drawings and specifications for small-scale fixture and furniture designs. These designs were sent to subscribers as promotional perks to supplement the array of available modern home plans. Our perforated, wall-mounted wood cabinet from the 48' House was featured for its simplicity and ease of construction.

Notes No. 2   149

2.04   The New American Home   2.06   54' Addition

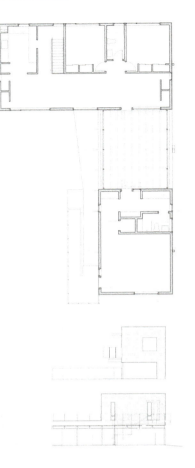

The 48' House was featured in a 2007
issue of *Dwell*, with photography by Daniel
Hennessey and text by Georgina Gustin.
Gustin's article foregrounds the influences
(and pressures) of building small in
Houston:

> *We like the challenge of having a
> big life in a small house*, says
> Wamble... Even Finley and Wamble—
> neither of whom are Texas-born—
> acknowledge they might need more
> space one day. The house is
> structured for a third story, and
> the lot could accommodate another
> building. But for now their
> compact home and workspace work
> perfectly in their non-Texan scale.

2.05   7.2 Panel

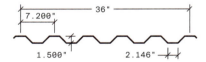

The corrugated-metal siding of
the [48'] house bestows another Houstonian touch. The material
is popular in the area because
it won't get moldy and rot in the
swampy air, and because it's
easy to maintain. But it's also
a local resource that evokes
the shotgun shacks and warehouses
of the city's pre-oil boom past.
*This is the metal building capital
of the country*, Finley says.
*So this material is coming off
the coil in Houston.*

—Georgina Gustin, 2007

In 2017 a significant addition to the 48'
House in Houston was completed. Designed to
include a range of new spaces—a master
suite, an acoustically separate office, and
a fabrication shop—the addition required
a steel structure to allow for the hoisting
of large machined parts and materials.
All architectural and structural steel was
designed, fabricated, and erected by
Interloop—Architecture.
    The ground floor is structured
with exposed, painted, architectural-grade
structural steel columns and beams
that organize the machine shop and carport. On the second level, a large outdoor
terrace separates the existing upper
residence from a new second-level office
suite. The addition is clad with a deep-
profile, corrugated, prefinished steel
7.2 panel, making the transition from old
to new seamless.

2.07   Steel Assembly

Our office served as the steel fabricator for all structural and architectural components to the 54' Addition. The precut, drilled, and painted structural beams were craned and set, then tightened down with bolt-hole tolerances within one-sixteenth of an inch. The final assembly took all of forty-five minutes.

2.08   DiverseWorks

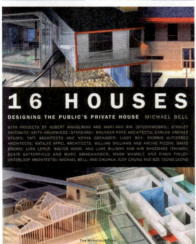

Interloop—Architecture was one of sixteen architectural firms invited to design single-family houses for the Fifth Ward Community Redevelopment Corporation in Houston. Initiated by the architect Michael Bell with support from the Graham Foundation, each of the designers was asked to speculate on the architectural implications of new federal policies of decentralization and dispersal. An exhibition of the projects, *16 Houses: Owning a House in the City*, opened in November 1998 at DiverseWorks in Houston before traveling to the University of Texas at Austin in the spring of 1999.

2.09   Federal Housing Vouchers

In the late 1990s, new federal and state housing initiatives provided financial assistance to qualified families and individuals in the form of housing "vouchers." The aid could be used only for the purchase of a house, which had to be occupied for a minimum of five years. The initiative not only created opportunities for affordable housing but equated ownership with representation, empowerment, and community.

> Quite often, the American dream home, with a gabled roof and shutters, becomes a symbol of success—so much so that the image of house precedes its performance and possibilities. The current financing structure and expected profit margins in low and moderate-income housing have come to limit the involvement of an architect. There is the assumption that the market is driven by a population that has little understanding or appreciation of what value design can offer; aesthetically or fiscally. Not so much lack of understanding as lack of exposure to other options; the 16 Houses initiative was an attempt to generate 16 innovative concepts for the house.

—Michael Bell, 2004

2.10   Sidestepping Conventions

In the 1950s, inventor Earl Tupper and saleswoman Brownie Wise pioneered a direct sales and distribution strategy for Tupperware, a then-unfamiliar line of plastic kitchen containers. Advances in material technologies after World War II allowed for the production of plastics that were safe for the consumer market. Wise recognized, however, that the radical departure from the familiar traditions of glass and ceramic would require an innovative sales system.

Through the now iconic *Tupperware party*, the company built a distributed sales workforce made up almost exclusively of upper-middle-class white women. A hostess would invite friends and neighbors to a party in her own home and demonstrate the Tupperware products, collecting orders and payment using a simple order form. In exchange for the use of her home and social network, the hostess received product gifts in addition to a commission.

This early example sidestepped the conventional channels of retail outlets, product sales, and distribution by directly engaging social networks, mediating product and service models to an inventive end. We continue to see this precedent as having critical potential for how architecture might be reconceived as a system of services rather than a system of parts.

2.11   Product/Service

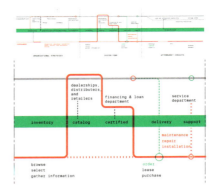

Examples of the house as a delivery platform are not new; however, until the limited, post-Great Recession rise in new housing models worldwide, architecture of the single-family house has endured as a system of goods (products) rather than a system of services. Klip situates the critical material components of a house within a larger network of ongoing consumer support—including advertisement, sales, participating manufacturers, financing, delivery, maintenance, upgrade, demanufacturing, and recycling. Klip was thus an early exploration of the more diverse array of housing emerging today.

2.12   Cuddletech

One of the first, if not the first, attributions of the term *cuddletech* was in 1998 by the journalist Shaila Dewan in her description of Interloop—Architecture's Klip project for the *Houston Press*:

> Many of the architects in the [*16 Houses*] show developed a modular system in which prefabricated units could be configured into different houses to meet different needs, but none so boldly as Mark Wamble and Dawn Finley. Embracing rather than eschewing the ways in which giant corporations shape our lives, they've envisioned a system in which familiar brand-name companies produce injection-molded modules that snap together on "Klip Binders" in the configuration of the client's choice. Therma-Rest manufactures a sleepklip, Igloo makes the chillklip, and Nike makes the hoopshoot attachment. It's pure cuddletech.

152   Procedure—Assembly

2.13 Press

In the 1990s, advances in material and manufacturing technologies were quickly integrated into product design, transforming the market for high-performance sports in particular. Architecture, or more specifically building design and delivery systems, was poised to take advantage of this context but slow to engage its potential. We researched consumer products and services, from automobiles to appliances to computers, looking at the material technologies, performance expectations, financing structures, warranties, and upgrades. We then organized these benefits around the acquisition and maintenance of a house.

  Klip, which received an *I.D.* design award, was covered extensively in the national and international press. It was included in *Less + More*, a publication by the Dutch curator Renny Ramakers, and in January 1999 was featured in a *Wall Street Journal* article titled "Just One Word: Plastics."

2.14 Verify in Shop

Extending our research on residential delivery, Plug-on is an eight-foot cube, fabricated entirely of stainless steel, glass, and wood. It is structured as a cantilever using a concrete counterweight and steel beam fulcrum underneath the bedroom floor. The project was the first in a series of product prototypes intended for residential structures. It was fabricated and assembled in Houston, then delivered and installed as an addition to a modest, one-story ranch-style house in Richardson, Texas. The client was interested in an addition that would complement the existing language of the house and accommodate a sitting area to redirect the space of the master bedroom to the lush trees in the rear lawn. Our directive was to maximize the qualitative effects of the space while adding very little square footage.

  Preparation of the existing structure, as well as interaction with local city agencies and landscape services, was provided by a contractor. All metalwork, mechanical systems, glazing, and interior finishes were fabricated off-site under our supervision, then coordinated, delivered, and installed by our office. This simple restructuring of existing contracting practices allowed our office to retain more control and responsibility for the critical material elements of the design, which ultimately kept the cost down, ensured quality, and maintained the schedule.

2.15 Assuming Risk

Innovation, like other impulses in the design field, is regulated. Professional institutions created to support architecture often undermine the proposal of structures, components, and elements that have no

Notes No. 2   153

common precedent. Most of the language contained in contracts associated with the construction industry deliberately avoids risk, a fundamental characteristic of innovation. There are circumstances that justify crossing the line between designer and fabricator, leaving the safety of the designer's realm and embarking upon the complexities and liabilities of the fabricator's world. By doing so we can recapture some of the innovative sensibility apparently written out of our discipline by insurance policies, professional associations, and institutions of higher learning.

—Dawn Finley, 2005

2.16 Polara 7

In addition to the Plug-on, we designed and fabricated a set of furniture for the client in Richardson, Texas. The unique stainless steel and wood pieces include a medicine cabinet, footlocker, side tables, and supply cart—each carefully calibrated to the human body and detailed with concealed fasteners on the outer surfaces. Stainless steel pieces were cut with a water jet and bent ninety degrees on a brake with a half-inch radius, then sanded with a nondirectional finish and sealed with a matte clear coat.

2.17 Pharmacy Futures

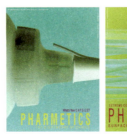

Pharmetics speculates on the future of retail pharmacies in the United States and how they will interrelate with a broad range of continually evolving systems, including healthcare regulations, insurance restrictions and reimbursements, market forces, and healthcare technologies. Scenario planning is used to project five extreme but plausible futures and to develop programming strategies for architectural speculation. The futures—titled Chain Exploit, Same Chains, Black Labs, Remote Dose, and Civic Response—stage speculative contexts for new forms of architecture to emerge.

Building, brand, service, and product strategies were developed for a hypothetical future pharmacy called "Pharmetics" using the Chain Exploit scenario (in 1999). *Investment in pharmaceutical research and technology continues to bring unlimited consumer choices through specialized manufacturing processes. Public demand for drugs and lifestyle benefits increase while costs and constraints skyrocket. Drugstore chains invest in specialized drug service centers for long-term economic self-interest. Chains use buying power, national recognition, and communication networking (with civic responsibility) to provide drugs, consultation, therapy, information services, compounding, and pharmacist-controlled drug experiments to the public.*

2.18 Slow Space

154   Procedure—Assembly

Architecture is an expression of economic force. That the discipline of architecture exists at all is evidence that potential wealth is in play; always searching for the next, and inevitable, augmentation of its material form. Indeed, no discipline of consequence, and no theory of architecture is comprehensive outside this base dynamic. Given recent shifts in economic practices, it should be of little surprise that productive strategies that once sustained comprehensive fiscal relationships between *building* and *city* have become reconfigured. Outmoded by its material and human connection to stable markets, the institution of *city* is compromised by a free-market system in transition, a transition defined by promiscuous forms of capital in search of the next play.

—Mark Wamble, 1998

2.19   Texas Ice House

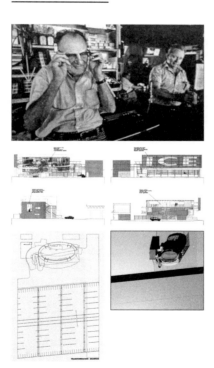

The case of the ice house demonstrates the legacy of conforming a bastard band of civility to the free-market system. In Texas, the ice house was originally a private commercial venture for the purpose of selling refrigeration. Two significant economic factors together elevated it to microeconomy status: the availability of the automobile in a sparsely populated, expansive landscape, and the mobile culture this created; and the unavailability of electricity in the rural outposts and fringe suburbs of the Southwest. Mobility combined with the cessation of domestic modernization sanctioned the ice house. By providing blocks of ice, a civil hybrid emerged that fulfilled both an important egalitarian, social need while instituting a public roadside gathering-place as important to Texans as the town common and city square vernacular of other regions. Although conceived as a private, commercial enterprise, the selling of ice also produced a collective forum, and the commercial elements of the ice house in turn thrived.

—Mark Wamble, 1998

2.20   Modified Procedures

Groundbreaking ceremonies for major public and civic projects traditionally involve politicians and financial donors. The participants gather on a site to take up shovels and turn the dirt, signifying the start of construction.

In 1962, at the groundbreaking ceremony for the Great Domed Stadium of Houston (today known as the Astrodome), members of the Houston Sports Authority drew Colt .45s and fired at the dirt. The stadium began life as an ambitious if eccentric proposal to house Houston's baseball team, the Colt .45s. After completion in 1965, the "Astrodome" hosted the team, renamed the Astros, in the first air-conditioned domed stadium, with a capacity of 50,000 spectators. Houston's hot, humid climate and open swamplands inspired the proposal. The image captures the entrepreneurial, Wild West attitude prevalent during Houston's early stages of development.

2.21   Design and Utility Patents

The U.S. Patent and Trademark Office offers two types of patents—utility and design—to innovators and designers. Claiming patents on most architectural work is challenging given the detailed aesthetic and performative specifications required by the office. Patent applications must be backed up with extensive research to prove that no preexisting, comparable articles exist—either on the market or in the world. That is, *novelty* is a legal requirement and one of the qualities tested to determine patent eligibility.

Utility patents cover how an article works and provide twenty years of protection. Design patents cover how an article appears or looks and provide exclusive rights protection for fourteen years. Through our company ASC, Mark Wamble has obtained one utility patent, three design patents, and one pending utility patent for the custom exit light, LELU.

2.22   R+D Award

LELU received a prestigious 2016 ARCHITECT R+D Award.

> Interloop—Architecture saw an opportunity to rework the much-begrudged object required in every building.

—Nate Berg, 2016

2.23   UL Listed

Underwriter Laboratories (UL) is a private agency with strict, some might say "arduous," constraints that often preclude design innovation. In addition to numerous material and manufacturing specifications, our prototype exit-light fixtures with free-floating letters were required to undergo a "Non-energized Contrast Visibility" test in which certified inspectors cut or clip the letter forms of one fixture to alter its legibility. The altered and original fixtures are then hung side-by-side in a 100-foot-long corridor. Both of the exit-light fixtures are then turned off and illuminated with an external thirty-foot candle light source. A test subject standing at the opposite end of the long corridor is then given ten seconds to identify which fixture is the complete, unaltered fixture containing all four letters, E, X, I, and T.

This test explains why most UL-approved fixtures are designed with a background surface that provides visual contrast. Our fixtures LELU and ELIS both passed this test and are listed in the United States and Canada by Underwriter Laboratories (UL 924).

2.24   Milled to Molded

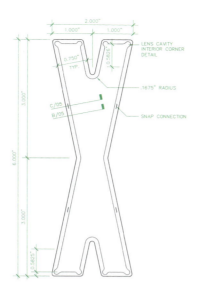

Manufactured injection-molded components require a huge investment of up-front capital for very little cost per piece — capital that our start-up did not have during the initial prototyping and UL testing phase for our custom exit light. Consequently, for the first years of production, LELU fixtures were assembled with precision milled acrylic lenses, more costly per piece but limited in quantity. After a few cycles of accrued revenue, and with the support of a handful of "angel" investors, five molds, milled and machined of solid aluminum, were designed and produced for the individual letters and chevron. LELU and ELIS fixtures now use identical snap-connector lenses, manufactured in Minnesota and produced with a custom green or a custom red polymer mix.

2.25   Architectural Precedent

A UL-approved custom exit sign is a rare object in the United States. Our research turned up only one example, designed as part of a building's graphics and signage package by the designer Lou Dorfsman for Eero Saarinen's 1965 CBS Building in New York City. Dorfsman customized the seventeenth-century typeface Didot for a series of graphic elements, including exterior and interior signage, floor and room numbers, mailbox slots, and custom exit signs. These opulent, top-mount, edge-lit exit signs with brass-coated letters were said to have been approved "over the protest, but final consent of the NYC Fire Department."

2.26   Forty-Six Fixtures

In 2003 we worked in collaboration with the graphic design firm 2x4 to develop concepts for a custom life-safety emergency exit fixture for the Nasher Sculpture Center in Dallas. Our office was then hired independently to research the technical constraints and to design and fabricate a limited run of forty-six fixtures for the museum. While the fixtures did conform to all UL guidelines, they were approved only for the Nasher installation and not for mass production. The fixtures required final approval and sign-off from the local Dallas fire marshal at the final building inspection. This intensive research endeavor allowed our office to make broad connections among fabrication processes, material and lighting technologies, industrial design, and legislative safety standards.

2.27   Museum of Modern Art

On November 7, 2007, the Museum of Modern Art (MoMA) in New York inducted our custom exit-light fixture into its permanent collection, providing an early precedent for the acquisition of architectural signage. The sign was exhibited for the first time in 2008-2009 in MoMA's third-floor Special Exhibitions Gallery along with an eclectic array of work by artists such as Gordon Matta-Clark, Marcel Duchamp, and Rachel Whiteread.

2.28   Transmaterial

Our custom fixture for the Nasher Sculpture Center was featured in *Transmaterial: A Catalog of Materials That Redefine Our Physical Environment*, edited by Blaine Brownell and published in 2006.

2.29   Design in Construction

We were hired by the Nasher Foundation from 2001 to 2003 to provide a wide range of design- and construction-related services for the Nasher Sculpture Center, a 50,000-square-foot museum in Dallas designed by Renzo Piano Building Workshop (RPBW), Genoa. Initially, the general contractor and architect of record for the project were one and the same. All parties eventually recognized this could lead to conflicts of interest during the construction phase. RPBW invited our office to serve as designers and design advocates for the design architect and client and to facilitate the implementation of their design. While this might seem like technical execution, it proved to be an unprecedented opportunity for invention, both subtle and overt.

Our experience on this project confirmed our long-held belief that the construction phase is one of the most creative phases of architectural design. No technical translation (i.e., execution) of an architectural design exists without creative synthesis and design thinking. Driven by economic incentives offered by the contractor, the groundbreaking and construction were brought forward so that the project commenced prior to the issuing of completed architectural construction documents. As a result, details, material components, and material assembly sequences were coordinated just-in-time, in the field, and in response to unexpected product and code-compliance requirements. While construction documents (coupled with specifications) are essential for communicating design intent, they are often incapable of anticipating the dynamic overlay of labor, raw materials, manufactured components, and performance criteria—even when these are issued prior to construction. Architects are thus instrumental in facilitating design throughout the construction process, navigating the diverse needs of the client, other consultants, and various ancillary constituents.

2.30   Global Practice

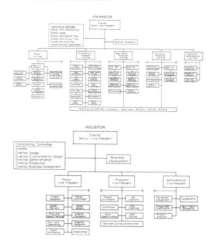

After World War II, when enormous innovations were made in communication and information management technologies, architectural practices began to engage more complex building problems—airports, laboratories, power plants—prompting the rise of national and multinational corporations that required the assembly and management of practice protocols. Not only were building design processes and sequences managed with almost scientific methods of analysis, but even the representational tools for design took on a more objective tone. Research was culturally equated with progress, shaping both the methods and the representations of architectural practice.

In the late 1950s, Welton Becket & Associates developed five organizational charts (two are shown above) to graphically organize the hierarchical lines of communication within their Los Angeles and Houston offices. This graphic type continues to be used by professional offices to explicate the organization of complex building project teams, often expanding to include the client, architect, engineers, and specialty consultants.

2.31   Cut and Paste

In 2001, the Nasher Foundation hired our office to produce images for a press release to be issued during the construction phase of the Nasher Sculpture Center. Producing the images required a negotiation between client and architect and was thus not a straightforward task. The client and the museum constituency wanted full-color renderings of the building and site that would generate national and international attention. RPBW's representation protocols, however, did not permit the use of computer-generated renderings or any form of digitally produced three-dimensional image, and thus their office would not produce the collection of immersive images requested by the client.

To mediate the client's need for images and the architect's policy against producing them, our office developed an inventive cut-and-paste technique, aiming for a new drawing aesthetic that reconciled digital and analog drawing processes. Each view and image was precisely structured using underlying line work generated from a digital model. Once each view was composed, we took on the meticulous, somewhat maniacal task of rendering large material surfaces, such as travertine or basalt, with varying light qualities, then cutting and placing individual panels in the drawings. We combined haptic, textured material surfaces and flat, bold color fills to situate images that flicker between a graphic cartoon and a renaissance painting. The images were then overlaid with vibrant trees, artwork, people, and shadows.

These drawing procedures and visual effects predate the postdigital representation experiments in architecture of the 2010s. We were looking for new design sensibilities through subtle interrogations of digital technologies.

Notes No. 2

2.32 Degrees of Alteration   2.33 Two-Seater

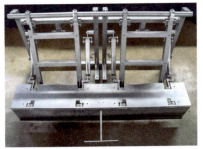

In addition to producing construction documents and attending weekly site visits with the client and consultant groups for the Nasher Sculpture Center in Dallas, our office was separately contracted to work with the landscape architects, the chef for the café, and the retail designer for the gift shop. We were hired to design all the furniture and architectural steel elements (to be reviewed by RPBW) and to independently produce the building enclosure for the James Turrell artwork, as well as custom exit lights for the museum interior.

    Implementing the various aspects of the Nasher project became our field of expertise, as everything was custom and the owner wanted the final result to be integrated and exceptional. Our office knew the project perhaps better than any other design office primarily because we worked closely with the owner, the artists, the design consultants, and the contractors on a daily basis and often on-site. None of the design work produced by the design consultants was integrated without some degree of alteration or redesign on our part. We were often asked to design new elements to make the project work as a whole. No part of the project accessible to the public was off-the-shelf. Everything was custom designed and fabricated.

Two-Seater is a folding bench armature that was engineered and fabricated by Interloop—Architecture for *Tending,(blue)*. The bench is a critical element for experiencing Turrell's skyspace artwork. Texas Accessibility Standards require that the bench accommodate wheelchair access for two individuals seated side by side. Instead of creating a void in the continuous bench for these seats, we developed a retractable armature that could support the required portion of the bench (over 400 pounds of stone cladding), enabling it to fold into the wall. Actuators allow an individual to operate the bench with little effort using a concealed handle to slide the bench into position or to fold it back into the wall.

No contractors or subcontractors wanted the responsibility or liability for constructing or installing such a kinetic infrastructural piece. No one had ever seen or heard of one before, let alone constructed one. Our office was thus contracted to design, fabricate, and oversee the installation of the armature, a responsibility we were happy to take on. Because the design and fabrication relied heavily on CNC processes, we were able to take the fabrication and construction steps of the project and subsume them into the design steps. That is, because the production parameters allowed for feedback, the formal documents describing the hinges, actuators, levers, and mounting points were updated throughout the fabrication process — a far more efficient and precise mechanism for creating such a highly engineered piece of equipment.

2.34 Light and Color

In 1991, Mark Wamble led an experimental seminar at Rice University School of Architecture titled Light and Color. Students studied the work of artist James Turrell and produced a two-part interactive space between Anderson Hall and Smith Courtyard. In addition to design research, Wamble and the students traveled to meet with the renowned artist and visited his infamous Roden Crater during its construction.

2.35 Obstructed Air

In 2012, the controversial Museum Tower was constructed in downtown Dallas, looming over the Nasher Sculpture Center site and obstructing the clear view of the sky from *Tending,(blue)*. Although Ray Nasher was said to have had a "gentlemen's agreement" with the real estate developers that the prospective tower not exceed twenty stories, after his death the luxury condominium was redesigned to be forty stories. Once built, the tower obstructed the view from *Tending,(blue)*, and Turrell declared his artwork destroyed. It has been closed to the public ever since.

Notes No. 2 161

Part 3

Material—
Detail

Material—Detail

170	Yoga Studio and Garden
192	Hempstead Research Center
214	J-Camp
238	Inside Corner
254	Notes No. 3

In our practice *material* is understood broadly as that which makes up the matter of architecture; it includes concrete, steel, wood, stone, and even paint but also the physical contingencies and consequences that these elements bring to bear within a given external context over time. Material is not static, nor is it abstract or neutral. It exerts structural, thermal, visual, and textural qualities and possesses less-corporeal economic and cultural attributes. All architecture, regardless of scale or complexity, sets into motion a system of interdependency and response with its context, natural or artificial, rural or urban. With this in mind, we value material's instrumentality in design, as well as its inherent indeterminacy in the world.

The rise of measured projection and perspective drawing techniques during the Renaissance ostensibly displaced the architect's role from that of someone with direct material expertise derived through making to that of communicator and coordinator of material relationships with fabricators and craftspeople. Drawing intervened, allowing the liberation and advancement of theory, increased abstraction, and an emphasis on precision (rather than the imperfections that materials often engender). The sustained, diverse impacts of this disciplinary division (between those who instruct and coordinate expertise and those who use that expertise to fabricate and assemble) cannot be understated and has been written about extensively in the past twenty years. However, in this context of supposed material displacement, our practice regards architectural details (both drawing and built artifacts) as critical design tools for engaging a range of material specificities to posit new potentials and effects in our work. Architectural details specify and coordinate the connections between materials and their finish, or treatment, and address an array of performance criteria in design (thermal, durable, aesthetic).

In architecture, the term *detail* refers both to a scaled drawing fragment that isolates a specific aspect of a larger material assembly and to a limited, manageable portion of the physical construction itself, built at one-to-one scale. (Architects sometimes use the word indiscriminately, as drawings and constructions are difficult to disentangle.) Details define material connections and expression at a range of scales. For most architects, engagement with material takes the form of drawing a detail.

In the United States and other industrialized nations, raw material has been revalued (and narrowly defined) through systems of distribution. That is, raw materials are (trans)formed into precise, discrete, and often repetitive standard units designed to coordinate with common building construction systems. Many instances of this coordination in various building types do not require architectural detail drawings, as the material relationships and supporting hardware or tools are standard practices of construction (e.g., a drawing that communicates the attachment of drywall to a steel stud is not necessary).

Material and *detail* are perhaps the two architectural terms that sit together most comfortably. Detail relies on material. Material is coordinated through detail, however precise or inexact. In our work, their mediation is essential to design, and we use details to amplify the conceptual premise of each project. The scale and role of details are fluid from project to project. Each project situates new opportunities for thinking through the architectural agency of details, whether formal, technical, or conceptual.

The following four projects—Yoga Studio and Garden (a private studio, terrace, and pool), Hempstead Research Center (an institutional building and strategic plan), J-Camp (a year-round campground campus), and Inside Corner (a private residence)—prioritize material in distinct ways while registering the elastic performance of detail in architecture. The first project engages more traditional methods of material composition and craft with technological advances that conflate detailing with pattern making. The second and third projects highlight the temporal impact of natural and artificial ecologies, where material interventions require the interdependency of site and building detail. The final project strategically calibrates the scale and position of materials sourced in domestic architecture, designing and organizing (presumably costly) architectural details to fall largely outside of a contractor's scope of work.

<u>Yoga Studio and Garden</u>

Yoga Studio and Garden, designed for the teaching and practice of traditional Mysore Ashtanga yoga, is sited within the rear yard of a 1920s bungalow in a historic neighborhood of Houston. The project sits among deep narrow lots with an array of tree canopies and gardens. The clients open their doors for practice at 4:30 a.m. almost every morning, allowing up to twenty-five students to quietly filter in and out of the space over a three-hour period for independent practice. Material is used strategically to spatialize, scale, and sequence the site—beginning with an elevated planted terrace that guides students past an existing bungalow and partially hidden pond-like swimming pool to an outdoor staircase that leads to a second-level studio space.

Few elements within the design used standard construction or installation details, and therefore numerous detail drawings and drawing types were produced to communicate our technical and aesthetic design intentions. Each material surface is detailed to amplify the qualities of the project's three primary architectural elements (studio building, pool, porch), which are connected by the elevated terrace. Surfaces are detailed to break down into repeating and nonrepeating (serial) patterns, with the aim of diffusing the discrete boundary of each object through a kind of material pixilation that visually correlates the independent elements (concrete planks, wood slats, brake-form steel panels).

The practice space is defined by floor-to-ceiling glass on three sides, overlooking the elevated terrace. Views and sunlight are filtered through a delicate custom hardwood screen that wraps the building exterior. The screen mediates the transition from the open space of practice to its surroundings through a precise, varied assemblage of three-quarter-by-one-and-one-half-inch pieces of dense Brazilian hardwood. The screen integrates variable density and spacing that subtly transform as it wraps the exterior steel staircase and building.

Our approach to detail in this project is both specific to the properties and limits of each individual material and generalized across the collective whole, with each instance designed to repeat and produce larger, recognizable patterned architectural surfaces. For the hardwood screen, traditional material craft is combined with digital technologies (computation) to produce new drawing formats and fabrication sensibilities. The methods of digital design and material production eliminate traditional, fixed, three-inch detail drawings, replacing them with instructional diagrams that communicate the assembly sequence; that is, additive relationships between each material member rather than a predetermined drawing composition. The resulting aesthetic sensibility of the screen's details and production influenced the treatment of most other materials within the project.

Hempstead
Research Center

The next project engages a dynamic site ecology as an integral part of a material strategy for the design of a landscape, formal garden, and institutional building. Hempstead Garden had occupied a nineteen-acre site in southeast Texas for more than thirty years when its newly formed conservation board acquired an adjacent twenty-acre property. Our office was commissioned to take stock of how the old and new sites were being used for work and leisure; to research the various systems (environmental, labor, social) that contributed to or enabled its operation; and to develop a site strategy for a garden and research center that could serve as a public educational and cultural destination.

We also produced a series of diagrams to study how a site strategy might affect the institution's development over time. These studies took into account required and speculative activities—for example, flood retention, irrigation, seed propagation, public programs, horticulture fellowships, and research—and their respective architectural supports. Concurrently, we developed diagrams of understory, intermediate, and upper canopy plant growth to understand how different durations and cycles, including germination, growth, reproduction, pollination, and seed spreading, might coincide with the growth of the institution. These dense, formal, and operational studies were essential to understanding the complex, reciprocal relationship between site and building.

Clad in weathered-steel rainscreen panels, the new building presents a simple, earthy, horizontal datum in the landscape, punctuated by a single vertical water tower used to survey the grounds and to harvest rainwater. The building is organized via a long circulation spine, flanked by a diverse array of public and private interior spaces and outdoor garden courtyards, both ornamental and scientific. Large glass entrances are tucked within the circulation spine so as not to be visible from the landscape. The weathered cladding is detailed to minimize the appearance of conventional building elements such as windows, doors, and downspouts. This lack of recognizable architectural elements makes it difficult to ascertain the size of the building in the landscape from a distance. Warm-hued cladding panels are perforated at strategic locations to allow natural light through large windows and into the interior spaces. The building details exploit scale (or lack thereof) to assert an attenuated, abstract background that allows the gardens to come in and out of focus, generating a reading that compares the building to the ground.

Architectural details are limited in their capacity to control or regulate how environmental conditions (natural or synthetic, anticipated or otherwise) will affect materials. Our selection of weathered-steel cladding panels sidesteps this issue, allowing for aesthetic effects that develop only over time. Detail drawings do not communicate effects but only dimensional relationships. The panels at Hempstead are detailed to direct rainwater, which is employed as an active material participant in the facade assembly and (in concert with the chemical composition of the air) changes the color, texture, and pattern of the building surfaces over time. In this case, we actively sought to use details to balance specificity and openness in the building's aesthetic evolution.

J-Camp

J-Camp is a year-round campground complex for inner-city kids run by a nonprofit organization in Dallas. Sited on a wooded peninsula within the 100-year flood-plain of one of the largest reservoirs in the United States, the site endures periodic, intentional flooding by the Army Corp of Engineers. On a typical day the site occupies 127 acres of land, but when flooded the land area shrinks to only thirty-six acres, a dramatic yet temporary transformation. Building in this context introduces new material cycles, interactions, and responses. Therefore, each architectural material was carefully selected for its performance and longevity.

The complex required a series of shared commons buildings (cafeteria, first aid, offices, and recreation) and twenty-five cabins for up to 250 campers and staff. Rather than avoid the floodplain, our design proposal locates most of the camp buildings directly in the lower, wooded, flood-prone areas, but elevated on piers. All vehicular access occupies the upper ground, leading to an elevated circular commons at the end of the peninsula. The commons, built up of rammed earth and retaining walls, is a vehicular turnaround and large open plaza to which all of the public buildings connect via elevated walkways. The cabins are sprinkled in the woods, to the north and south of the road, allowing for dramatic views and breezes from the waterfront.

We developed a set of adaptable design guidelines to address the range of building types required for the camp. Each building uses a select number of repeatable, scalable building modules that aggregate to form large and small, public and private structures built using conventional two-by-six wood framing methods. The modules are sometimes composed into functional clusters and can be manipulated to generate formal and spatial diversity. For example, on one side of a building a module (or part of the building) may be oriented to capture a view of the lake, while a module on the other side of the building rotates slightly to connect with a walking path, open toward a prevailing breeze, or allow its occupants to take in a summer sunrise through a balcony opening. The result is a functional, visually playful series of colorful building shapes nestled in the trees and perched on elevated footings above the ground.

Each building maintains consistent construction details yet varies in proportion, size, height, orientation, and roof slope. Geometric rules in plan and section accommodated the inevitable need to adjust a building footprint on-site after trees, surface grade conditions, and views were verified. Familiar material building systems were appropriated and detailed with modest modifications that allowed volunteer crews to easily engage with construction systems under the supervision of a contractor. Details are systemic and pliable.

Inside Corner

The final project, Inside Corner, is a one-story residence with an expansive interior and series of gardens in Houston. The shared social spaces of the house are open and continuous with one another, visible and accessible through a lush, central, open-air planted courtyard. The residence is sited on an urban corner lot and faces inward, like a compound. A long, broad, opaque wall—covered with climbing bines and vines—defines the west elevation, which faces a busy street. Behind the wall is a series of small gardens that buffer bedroom spaces from the urban context. In contrast, the front entry allows a generous view across and through the interior courtyard—a graphic punctuation to an otherwise unassuming facade. The courtyard's foliage partially screens the domestic activity while allowing visual access to the layered interior.

In our experience, residential construction relies heavily on individual trades to resolve and coordinate material assemblies in the field. Architectural detail drawings are often produced to identify exceptions to conventional methods of construction, offering new material relationships or connections. In a house design, it is not uncommon for the kitchen and master-suite cabinetry to require a collection of details for their specialized construction. However, beyond that, sheets of three- and six-inch detail drawings, produced by the architect and issued to a residential contractor, often translate to increased construction costs, regardless of the details' complexity. Detail drawings signal a procedural change in workflow and potential changes to the construction schedule.

Our design for the Inside Corner house sidesteps this effect by rethinking details categorically—for example, by sorting architectural steel elements so they fall under our contract coordination (to include design, fabrication, delivery, and installation). Details, or exceptions to standard methods of construction, are designated as ornamental steel elements coupled with the strategic use of vibrant wall and cabinetry paint (a subtle yet effective graphic organizer that falls within the contractor's scope). This approach to details allows residential construction crews to work within the standards of their given trade while more specialized elements are drawn and fabricated independently, then coordinated and installed to meet the standard details.

Most other architectural materials within the scope of the contract, both interior and exterior, were selected to serve as modest, somewhat neutral backgrounds. The white stucco exterior, white gypsum interior walls, white subway tile, and white terrazzo flooring flecked with marble chips produce vast, open spaces and surfaces that highlight the articulated architectural objects: custom steel elements and built-in cabinets with chromatic interiors—not to mention the vibrant plant material visible from within the house. The glazed courtyard's vertical steel mullions, the steel entry gate's perforated stainless panels, the subtle gray of the kitchen cabinetry, and the built-in tequila bar's bright green painted surfaces collectively constitute a shift in the scale of details from that of material joins to that of spatial assemblies; that is, details that operate at the scale of a room.

Each project in our practice defines an approach to material through detail, positing or connecting a design ambition, however subtle, to the specificity of construction, coordination, and assembly. Technical proficiencies that continue to evolve through the revision and reiteration of known, studied details, in addition to experimentation with new details, are vital to the advancement of our practice.

Material—Detail

Yoga Studio and Garden

Client: Nystrom & Hardenbol
Dates: 2007-2011
Location: Houston, Texas

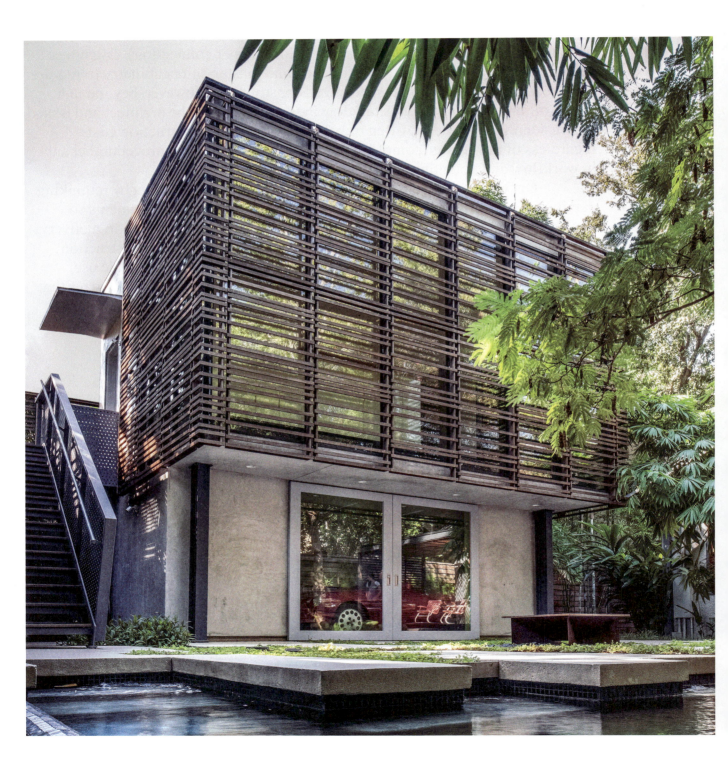

170 Material—Detail

The project presents densely packed unique materials and details—collectively producing a pattern-pixilation that visually connects the discrete architectural objects on the site.

Designed for the teaching and practice of traditional Mysore Ashtanga methods, the yoga studio is sited behind a 1920s airplane-style bungalow in Houston. The project sits among deep, narrow lots, packed with a diverse array of residential structures, tree canopies, and gardens. The pool, porch, and two-story building are connected to the residence through an open, elevated terrace, designed as a series of staggered, sandblasted concrete planks interspersed with planting beds for indigenous plant species. This open space links all new design elements at the ground level of the site, including a hardwood porch attached to the bungalow, a pond-like ornamental pool, sliding glass doors that access a garage/outdoor room, and a steel staircase that leads to the yoga studio above. The project presents densely packed unique materials and details—collectively producing a pattern-pixilation that visually connects the discrete architectural objects on the site.

At the second level, an open practice space, with floor-to-ceiling glass on three sides, overlooks the elevated terrace. Views and sunlight are filtered through a delicate custom hardwood screen that wraps the exterior of the building. The screen mediates between the open space of practice and the dense urban surroundings. It is composed of a precisely varied assemblage of three-quarter-inch-by-one-and-one-half-inch pieces of ipe, a dense Brazilian wood. The screen integrates various densities and patterns that subtly transform as it wraps the building exterior and exterior steel staircase.

Details in the project are specific to each material, its properties, and limits—brake-form steel, cast-in-place concrete, wood, natural stucco, ceramic tile—operating at a small scale while aggregating to produce larger, recognizable patterned architectural surfaces. For the hardwood screen, traditional material craft is combined with digital technologies (computation) that produce new drawing formats and fabrication sensibilities.

Yoga Studio and Garden

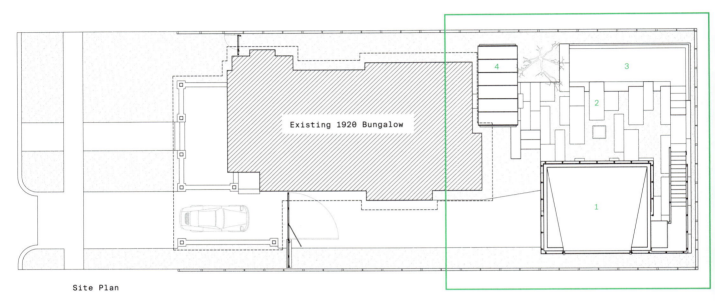

Site Plan

1 Two-story studio building
2 Terrace and planted garden
3 Pool
4 Covered porch

Yoga Studio and Garden 173

Screen Opacity and
Noise Study

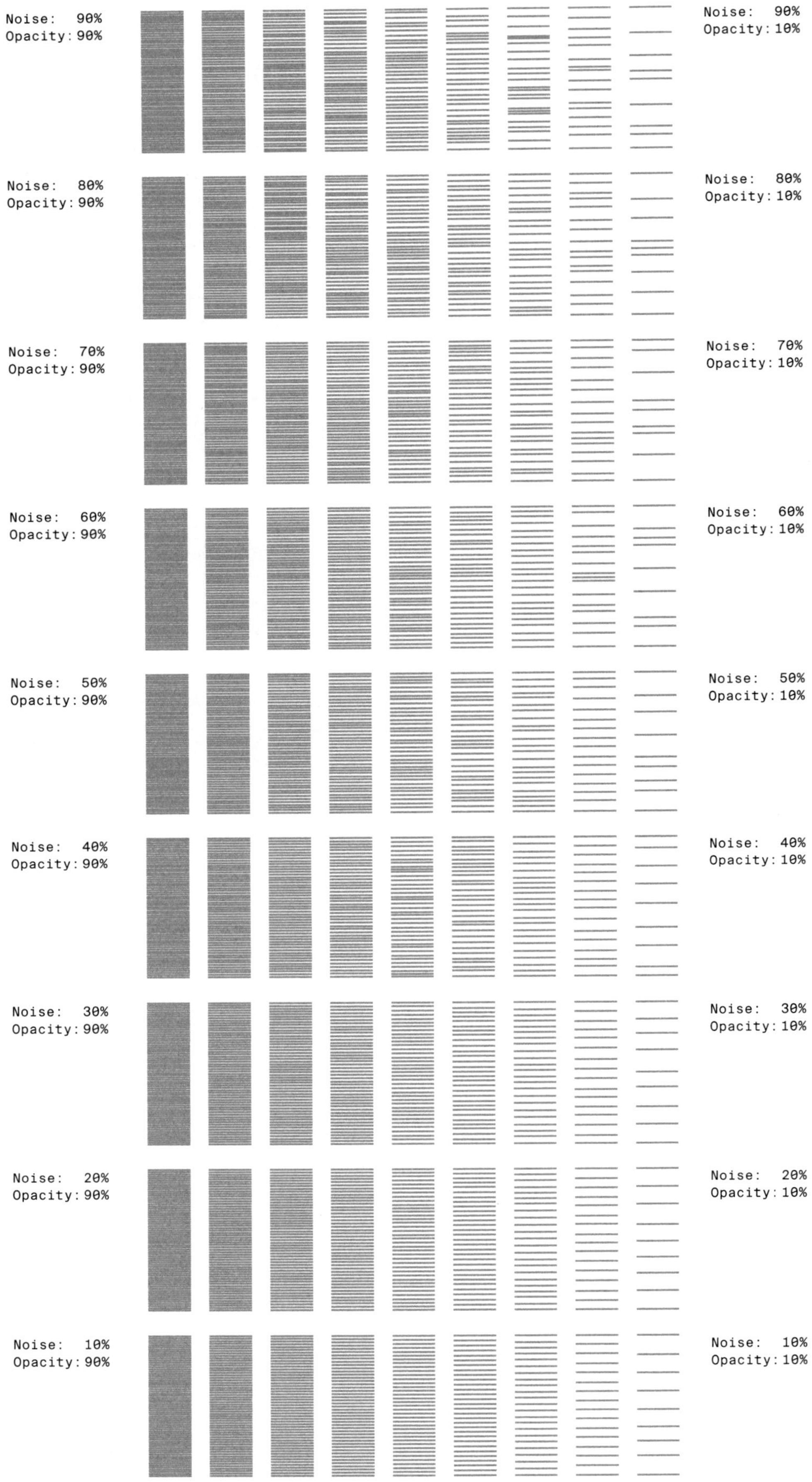

Noise: 90%
Opacity: 90%

Noise: 90%
Opacity: 10%

Noise: 80%
Opacity: 90%

Noise: 80%
Opacity: 10%

Noise: 70%
Opacity: 90%

Noise: 70%
Opacity: 10%

Noise: 60%
Opacity: 90%

Noise: 60%
Opacity: 10%

Noise: 50%
Opacity: 90%

Noise: 50%
Opacity: 10%

Noise: 40%
Opacity: 90%

Noise: 40%
Opacity: 10%

Noise: 30%
Opacity: 90%

Noise: 30%
Opacity: 10%

Noise: 20%
Opacity: 90%

Noise: 20%
Opacity: 10%

Noise: 10%
Opacity: 90%

Noise: 10%
Opacity: 10%

Material—Detail

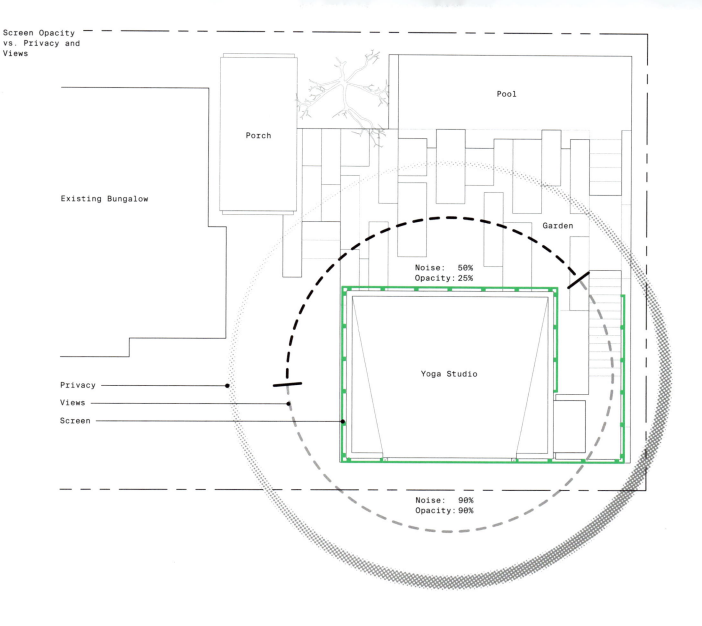

Yoga Studio and Garden

Partial Computational
Script

```
global proc float[] Noise_Panel(string name, float width, float height, float
unitHeight, float minimumGap, float atomLength, float noise, float opacity, float x,
float y ,float z, int notate){

float spacerList[];

float possibleGapHeights[];
int storageGapHeights[];
float maxOpacity =   unitHeight*( 1 +   (height - unitHeight)/(minimumGap +
unitHeight))/height;

float targetOpacityHeight = opacity*height;
int numSlats = (targetOpacityHeight/unitHeight);
float heightTransparent = height - targetOpacityHeight;
float remainder = heightTransparent/atomLength;
float totalSlatHeight = numSlats*unitHeight;
float totalTransparentHeight = height - totalSlatHeight;
float averageGap = totalTransparentHeight/(numSlats - 1);
float minGap = averageGap*(1 - noise);minGap = minGap - minGap%atomLength;
float maxGap = averageGap*(1 + noise);maxGap = maxGap + (atomLength -
maxGap%atomLength);
float ratioOpacity = (totalSlatHeight/height);
if(minGap < minimumGap){
minGap = minimumGap;
}
if(averageGap < minGap){
return(spacerList);
}
else{
possibleGapHeights[0] = minGap;
int count = 1;

do{
possibleGapHeights[count] = minGap + count*atomLength;
count++;
}hile(possibleGapHeights[count - 1] < maxGap);
float tenativeTransparentHeight = 0;
for(i = 0; i < numSlats - 1; i++){
storageGapHeights[i] = rand(0,count);
spacerList[i] = possibleGapHeights[storageGapHeights[i]];
tenativeTransparentHeight += possibleGapHeights[storageGapHeights[i]];
}

float heightDifference = totalTransparentHeight - tenativeTransparentHeight;
if (heightDifference > 0){

do{
int randomGap = rand(0,numSlats - 1);
if(storageGapHeights[randomGap] != (count - 1)){
storageGapHeights[randomGap] = storageGapHeights[randomGap]  + 1;
heightDifference = heightDifference - atomLength;
spacerList[randomGap] = spacerList[randomGap] + atomLength;
}
} while (heightDifference > 0);
```

N   Noise
O   Opacity
Mn Minimum Spacing
Mx Maximum Spacing

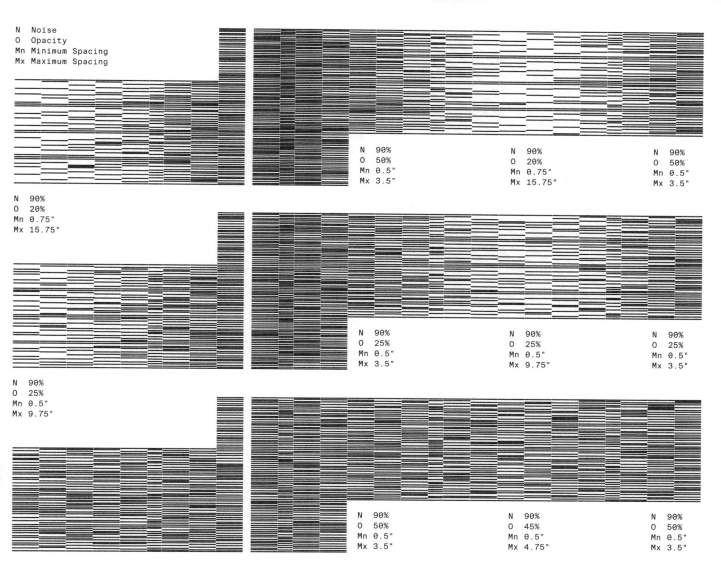

N   90%
O   20%
Mn 0.75"
Mx 15.75"

N   90%
O   50%
Mn 0.5"
Mx 3.5"

N   90%
O   20%
Mn 0.75"
Mx 15.75"

N   90%
O   50%
Mn 0.5"
Mx 3.5"

N   90%
O   25%
Mn 0.5"
Mx 9.75"

N   90%
O   25%
Mn 0.5"
Mx 3.5"

N   90%
O   25%
Mn 0.5"
Mx 9.75"

N   90%
O   25%
Mn 0.5"
Mx 3.5"

N   90%
O   50%
Mn 0.5"
Mx 3.5"

N   90%
O   45%
Mn 0.5"
Mx 4.75"

N   90%
O   50%
Mn 0.5"
Mx 3.5"

Unfolded elevation screen
studies, opacity, and
noise patterns developed with
computational scripts

Physical Model Studies:
Screen Opacity (O) vs. Noise (N)
Start: O = 0.5   N = 0.9
Finish: O = 0.3   N = 0.9

Physical Model Studies:
Screen Opacity (O) vs. Noise (N)
Start: O = 0.5   N = 0.001
Finish: O = 0.3   N = 0.7

Yoga Studio and Garden

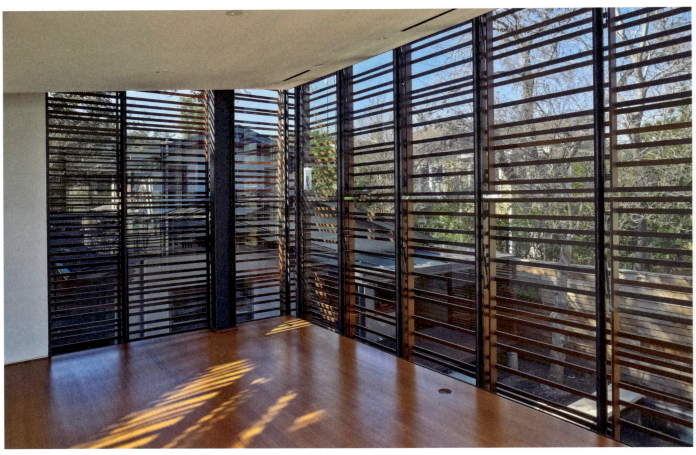

Material—Detail

Building, Garden, and Pool Section

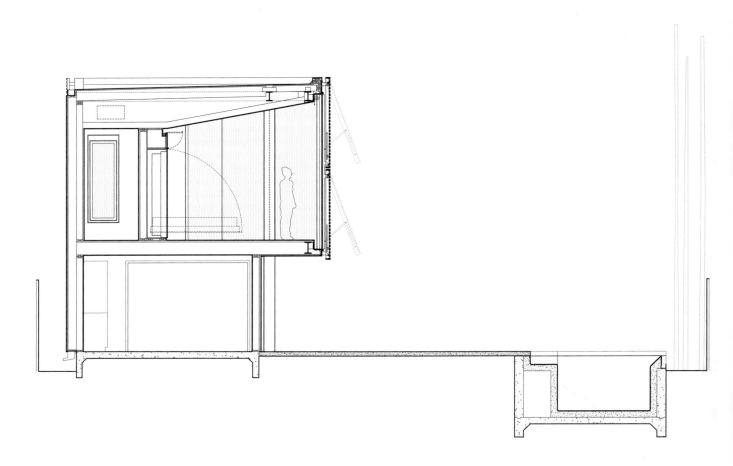

182 Material—Detail

Building Section

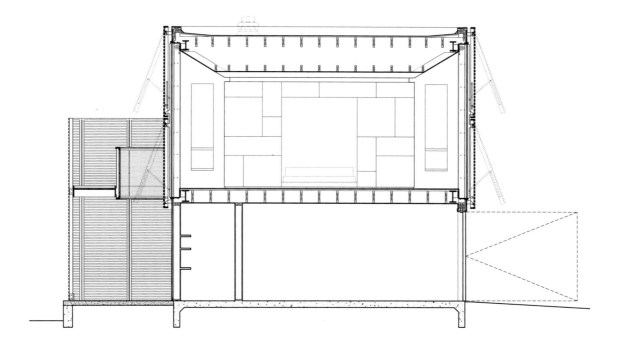

Yoga Studio and Garden

First Level Floor Plan:
garage/outdoor room,
laundry, and storage.

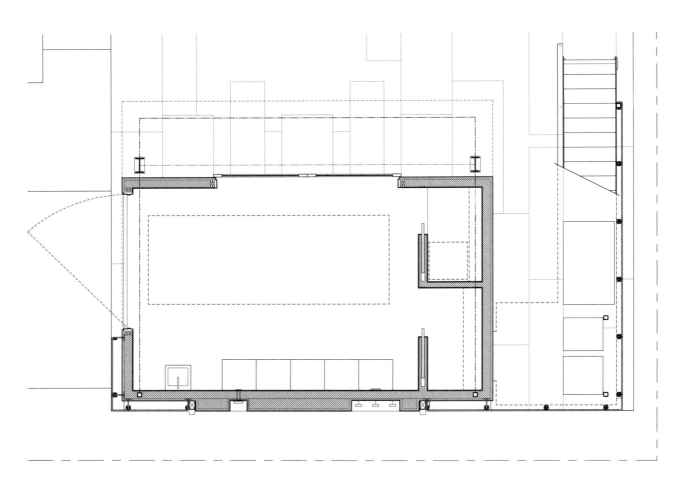

184   Material—Detail

Second Level Floor Plan: yoga studio/guest room, bathroom, shower room, and storage area.

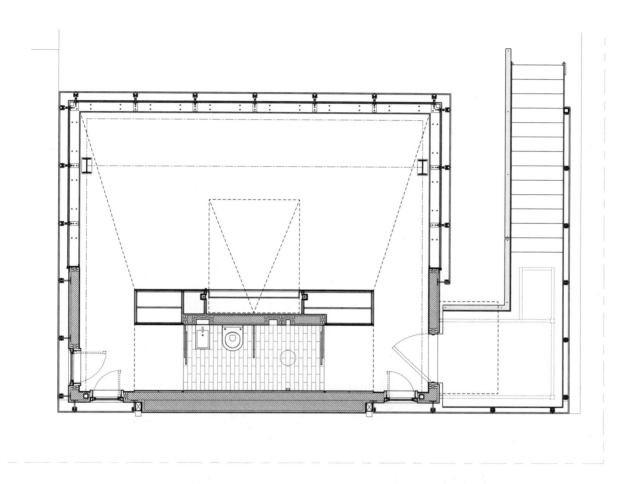

Yoga Studio and Garden

Yoga Studio and Garden

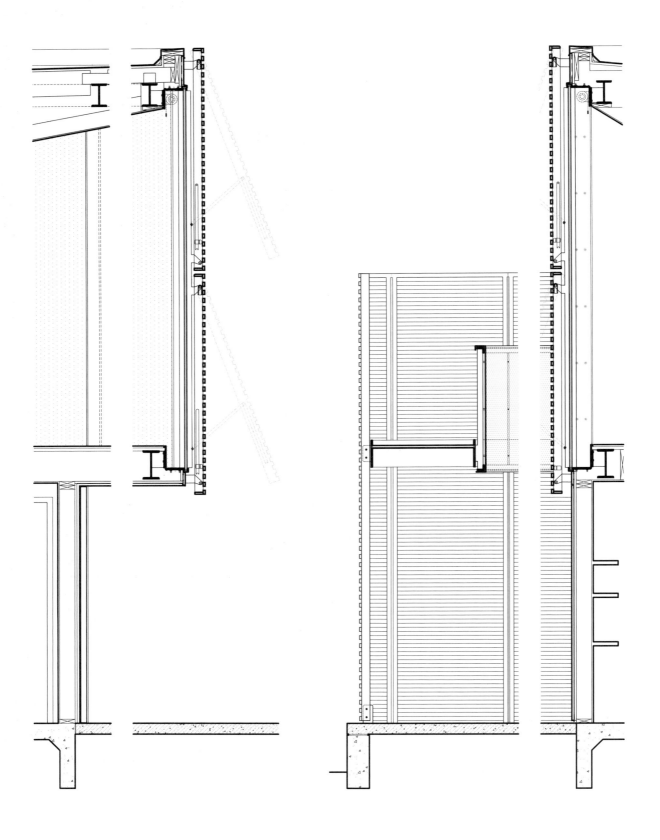

Wall sections at operable hardwood screens (left) and exterior stair (right)

188 Material—Detail

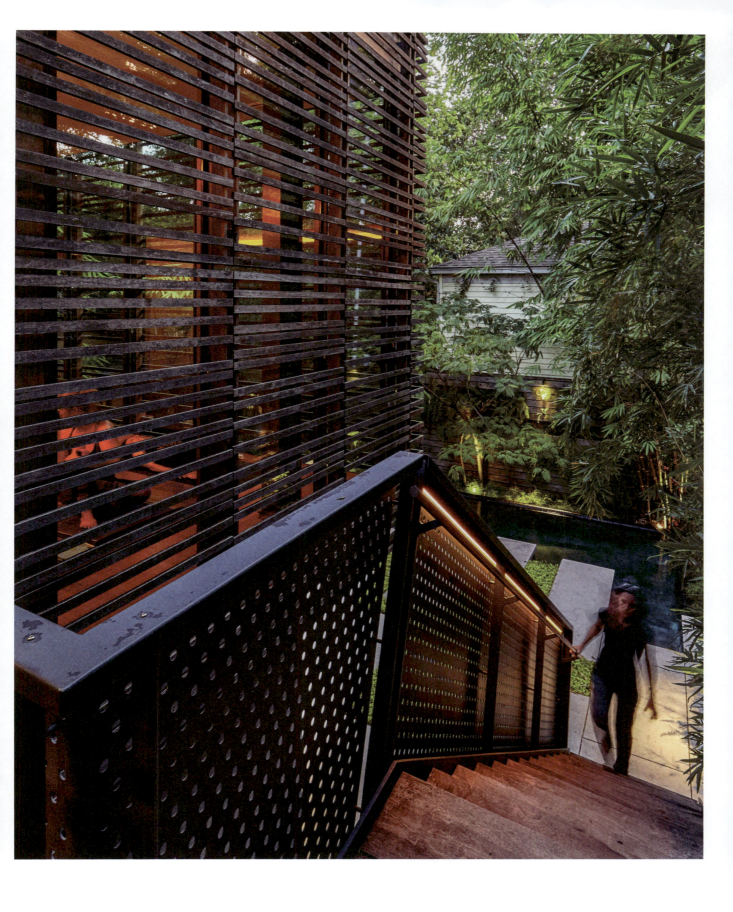

Yoga Studio and Garden

Custom hardware designed and fabricated for operable hardwood screens

Custom painted aluminum pivot door

Hempstead Research Center

Client: John Fairy Garden Conservation Foundation
Dates: 2010-2011
Location: Hempstead, Texas

192 Material—Detail

The courtyards appear as planted rooms: formal demonstrations of the research center's plant propagation and conservation efforts.

The property, a prominent private garden and residence on a nineteen-acre site in Hempstead, Texas, was owned and developed for more than thirty years by John Fairy, a professor of architecture at Texas A&M University. Prior to his death, Fairy established the garden conservation foundation that inherited the garden and acquired the adjacent twenty-acre property. The expanded property is located between two horticultural regions—the tropical wooded region of southeast Texas and the arid desert region of west Texas. The lower elevations of the original garden site to the north are cool and moist, while the upper contours of the site are warmer and more arid, with sandy soil composition. The significant variation in soil and plant types across the property has led to intense interest in experimentation and conservation. Our office was commissioned to design a site strategy to integrate the two properties, with the aim of forming a new landscape and research center to serve as an educational and cultural destination.

The design proposes an expansion of the formal garden onto the new property and provides a single, unified building infrastructure for plant research and propagation, cataloging

and storage of seeds, public educational activities, exhibitions and lectures, living accommodations for researchers in residence, administrative offices, and parking. Our garden design strategy distributes a series of new retention ponds and modest berms on the higher elevations of the garden, deliberately staging a collection of rare, regionally unique plants with varying growth cycles around and between the ponds. Types of plants include those that prefer the understory, the intermediate canopy, or the upper canopy.

Visually and acoustically buffering the county road and clad in weathered-steel exterior panels, the architecture presents a bold, horizontal datum in the landscape. The low, monolithic object is punctuated by a single vertical water tower used to survey the grounds and to harvest rainwater. Its attenuated elevation and material sensibility are commensurate with the expansive landscape. The building harbors an assemblage of private and public interior spaces, along with a series of outdoor ornamental and scientific garden courtyards. The courtyards appear as planted rooms: formal demonstrations of the research center's plant propagation and conservation efforts.

Porous groundscapes

Tree diversity

Hempstead Research Center

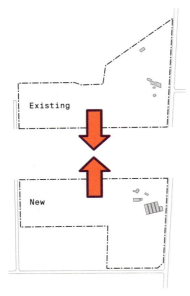

Union of Two
Properties

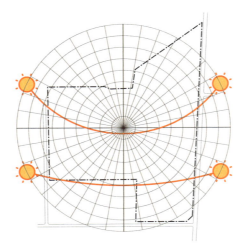

Summer and
Winter Solstices

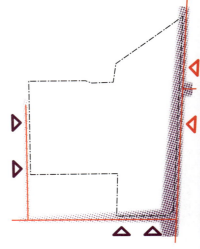

Vehicular
Noise and Access
Points

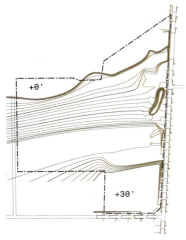

Topography

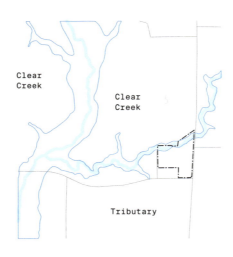

Floodplain Zone

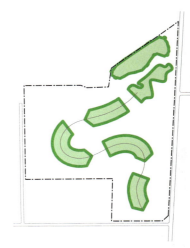

Canopy

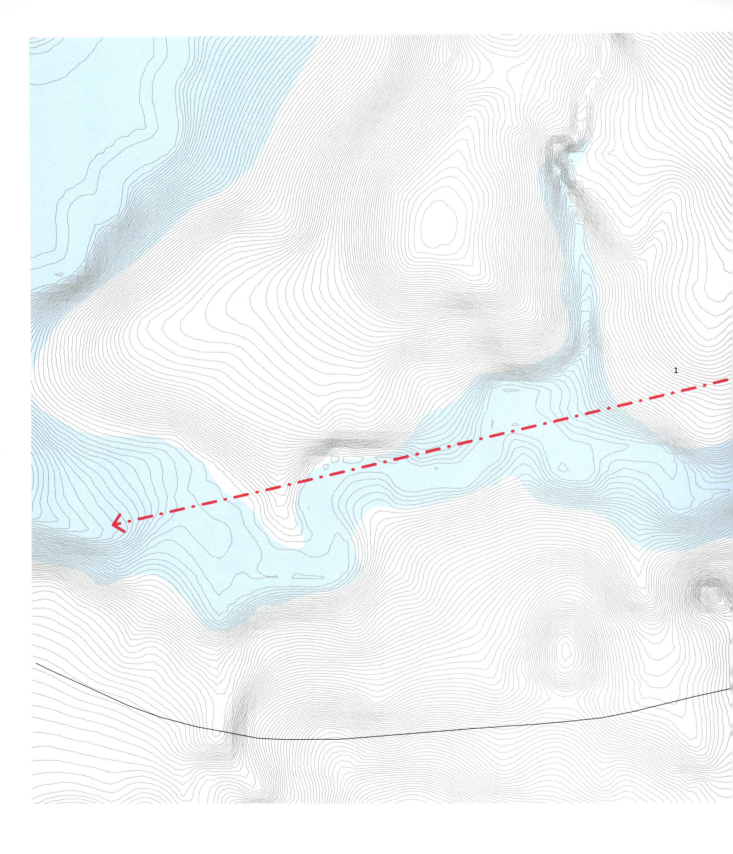

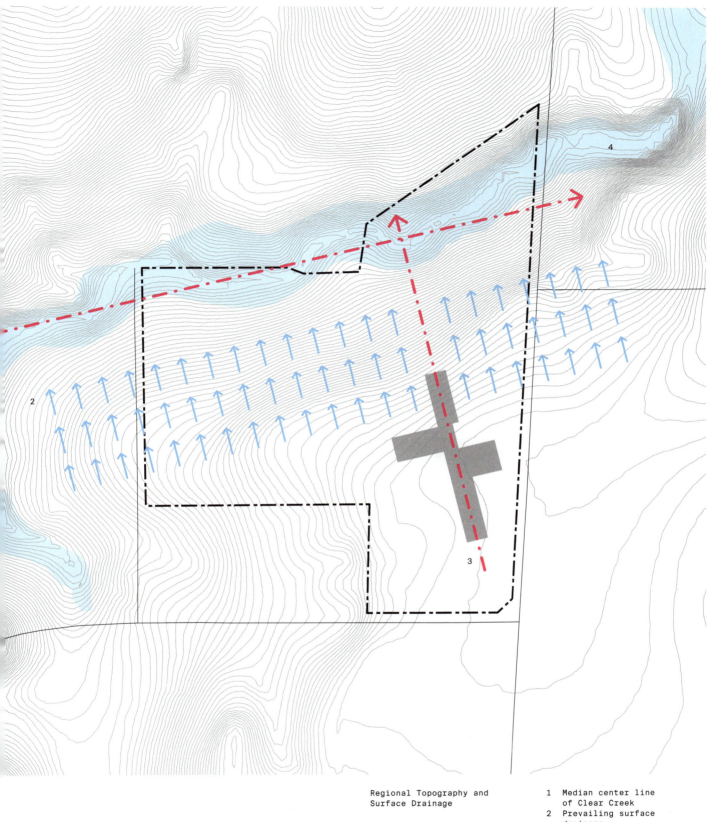

Regional Topography and Surface Drainage

1 Median center line of Clear Creek
2 Prevailing surface drainage
3 Proposed building and axis
4 Clear Creek Tributary

Hempstead Research Center

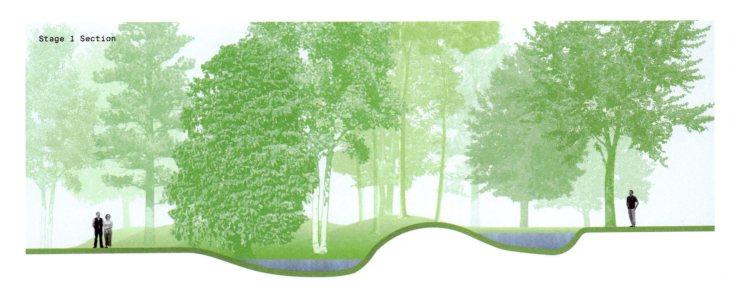

Stage 1	Upper Canopy Development
Stage 2	Intermediate Canopy Development
Stage 3	Understory Development

Stage 1 Plan Detail

Stage 2 Plan Detail

Stage 3 Plan Detail

N

Hempstead Research Center

Perspective diagram of retention ponds, water flow, and planting development

1. Upper Canopy Development, Phase 1
2. Intermediate Canopy Development, Phase 2
3. Understory Development, Phase 3
4. Sheet flow from southern end of property is directed to upper-level retention ponds.
5. Overflow from upper-level retention ponds is directed to lower-level retention ponds.
6. Sheet flow is directed to Clear Creek Tributary.

Building cross section at visitor center

Hempstead Research Center

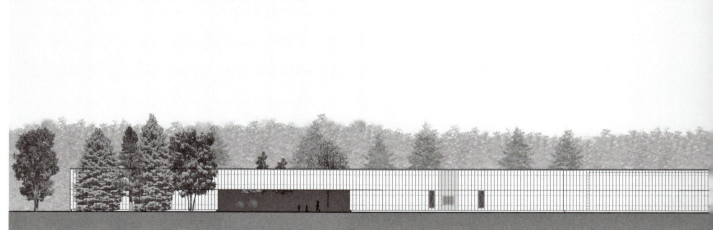

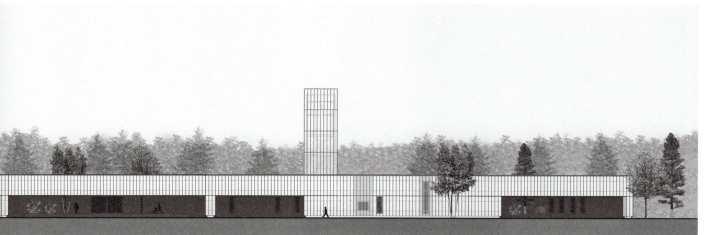

Top image: Exterior view of visitor center and flood retention ponds

Bottom image: East building elevation

Hempstead Research Center 205

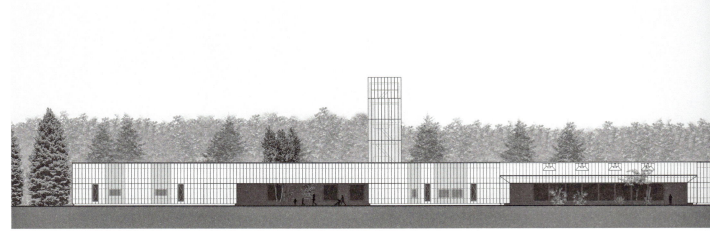

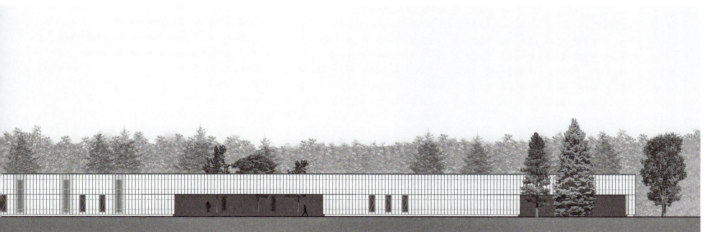

Top image left: View of exterior main corridor and courtyard with visitor center beyond

Top image right: Exterior view of courtyard

Bottom image: West building elevation

Hempstead Research Center

Stormwater Retrieval
and Irrigation Diagram

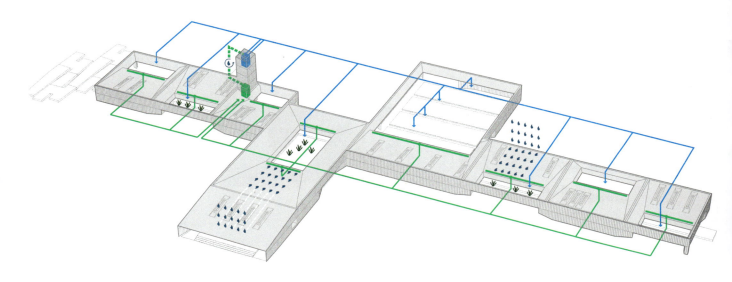

- 💧 Rainwater
- 🌱 Planting
- 💧 Water pump
- ▬ Rainwater collection
- ▬ Irrigation water

208   Material—Detail

Building Plan

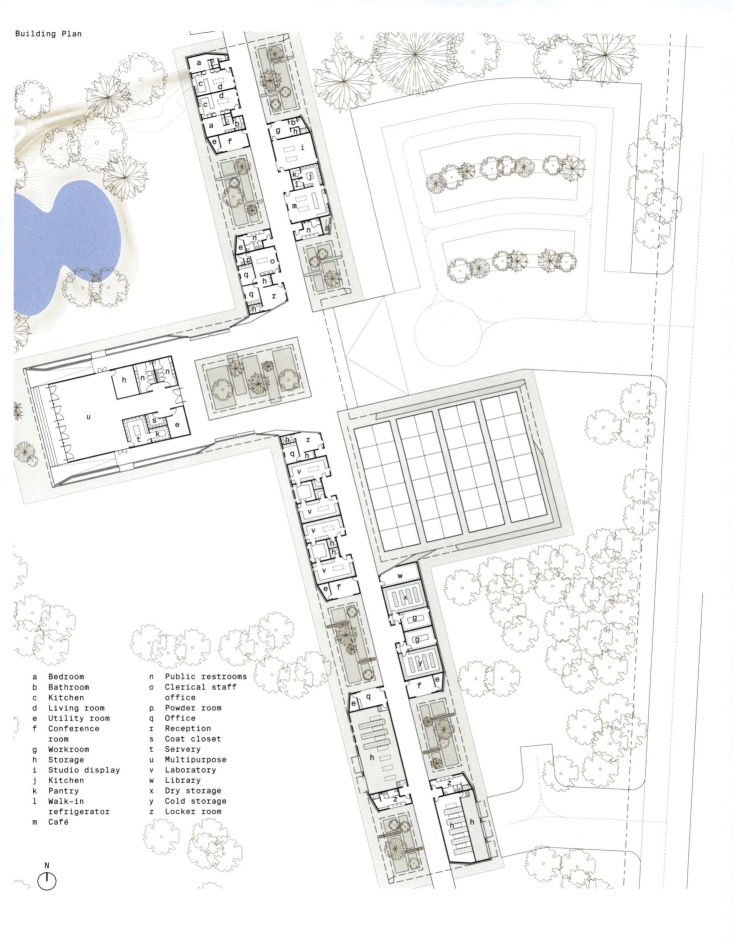

a Bedroom
b Bathroom
c Kitchen
d Living room
e Utility room
f Conference room
g Workroom
h Storage
i Studio display
j Kitchen
k Pantry
l Walk-in refrigerator
m Café
n Public restrooms
o Clerical staff office
p Powder room
q Office
r Reception
s Coat closet
t Servery
u Multipurpose
v Laboratory
w Library
x Dry storage
y Cold storage
z Locker room

Hempstead Research Center

Evening and afternoon views of rainscreen

Material—Detail

Rainscreen System
Assembly

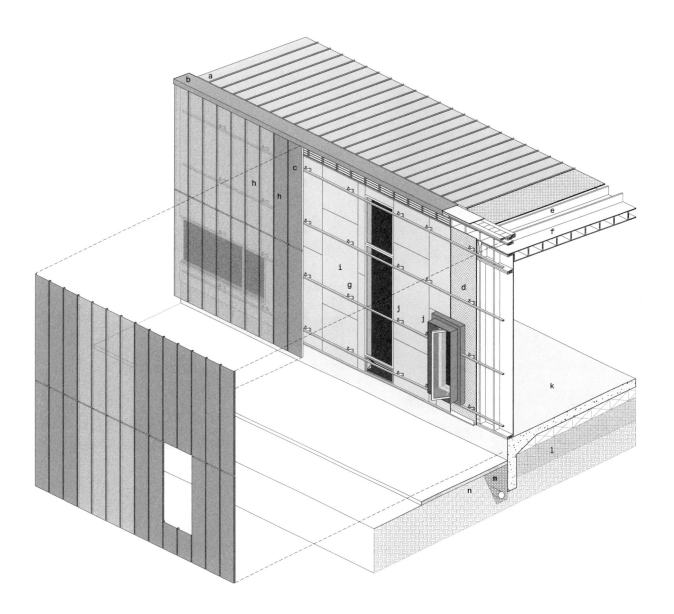

a   Prefinished standing seam metal roof
b   A606 ventilated light-gauge metal coping to ventilate roof and wall cavities
c   Premanufactured aluminum louver to ventilate roof cavity
d   Sheathing
e   Roof cavity framing
f   Structural roof framing
g   A588 steel brackets to support rainscreen
h   A606 rainscreen panels, solid and perforated to allow light, views, ventilation
i   HardiePanel, commercial grade
j   Preassembled thermally broken extruded aluminum windows, fixed and casement
k   Structural concrete slab
l   Select backfill
m   Perimeter drain
n   Existing soil

Hempstead Research Center

Exterior view of walkway
to existing gardens
and visitor center beyond

Hempstead Research Center

J-Camp

Client   Private
Dates   2013–2015
Location   Lake Texoma, Texas

J-Camp is a year-round campground complex on Lake Texoma, Texas. Each year it hosts up to 250 inner-city kids from the Dallas–Fort Worth metropolitan area. The lush site is a peninsula located within the 100-year floodplain of one of the largest reservoirs in the United States. The periodic, intentional flooding of the site by the Army Corp of Engineers creates a dramatic yet temporary transformation. On a typical day the site takes up 127 acres of land, but when flooded it drops to only thirty-six acres.

     The diverse technical and environmental challenges of the project—flooding, climate, buildable land area, geotechnical engineering, and structure—were researched in painstaking detail. After multiple iterations making broad and specific connections between technology and the environment, the proposal located all twenty-five sleeping cabins directly in the wooded floodplain, but elevated on piers—a radical departure from the client's understanding of the site's potential. The commons buildings, sited just above the 100-year floodplain, engage an engineered surface that is built up of rammed earth and retaining walls while taking advantage of the dramatic views and lake access.

Geometric rules in plan and section accommodate the inevitable need to adjust a building footprint on-site after trees, surface-grade conditions, and views are verified.

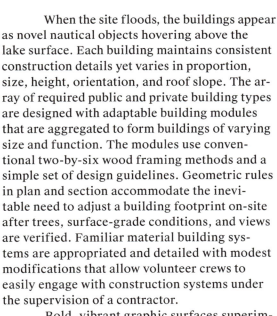

When the site floods, the buildings appear as novel nautical objects hovering above the lake surface. Each building maintains consistent construction details yet varies in proportion, size, height, orientation, and roof slope. The array of required public and private building types are designed with adaptable building modules that are aggregated to form buildings of varying size and function. The modules use conventional two-by-six wood framing methods and a simple set of design guidelines. Geometric rules in plan and section accommodate the inevitable need to adjust a building footprint on-site after trees, surface-grade conditions, and views are verified. Familiar material building systems are appropriated and detailed with modest modifications that allow volunteer crews to easily engage with construction systems under the supervision of a contractor.

Bold, vibrant graphic surfaces superimposed onto the buildings are critical to the camp's visual and wayfinding experience. The graphic boundaries are designed not to coincide with the exterior rainscreen cladding joints (which form a vertical running bond pattern). In particular, the application of razzle-dazzle, a two-dimensional graphic pattern applied to World War I ships for camouflage, on the public commons buildings, deliberately rescales and abstracts the building forms in the wooded landscape. This natural wooded environment with open expanses of water prevails as the dominant feature of the camp. As a counterpoint, the buildings' vibrant chromatic patterns pop intermittently into view then disappear behind the trees. Graphic differentiation of the buildings is especially important for the cabins, which are rarely seen as a collection.

J-Camp

Pliable Details Diagram

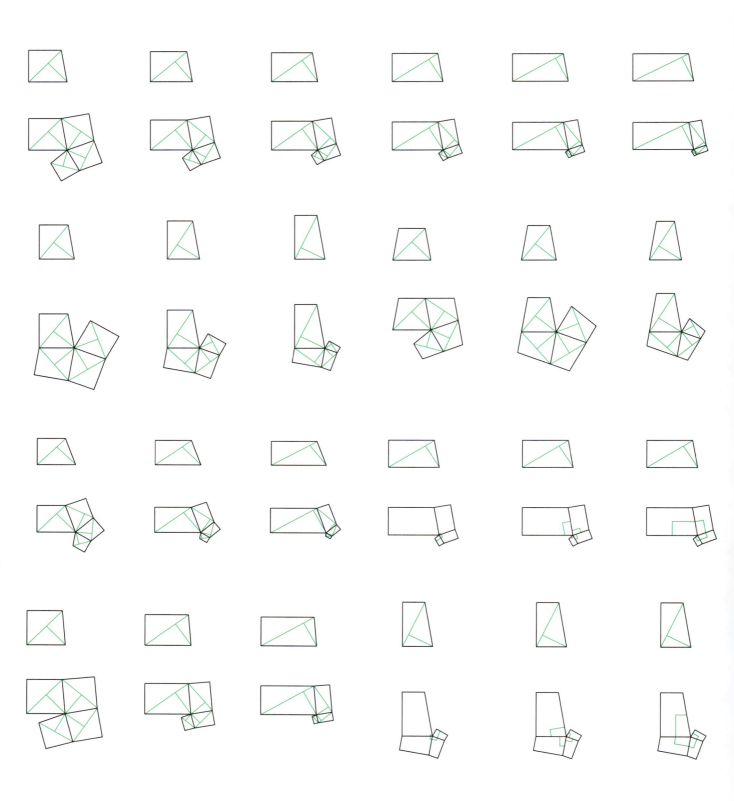

216 Material—Detail

Each cabin has a unique graphic and color combination for wayfinding in the wooded campground.

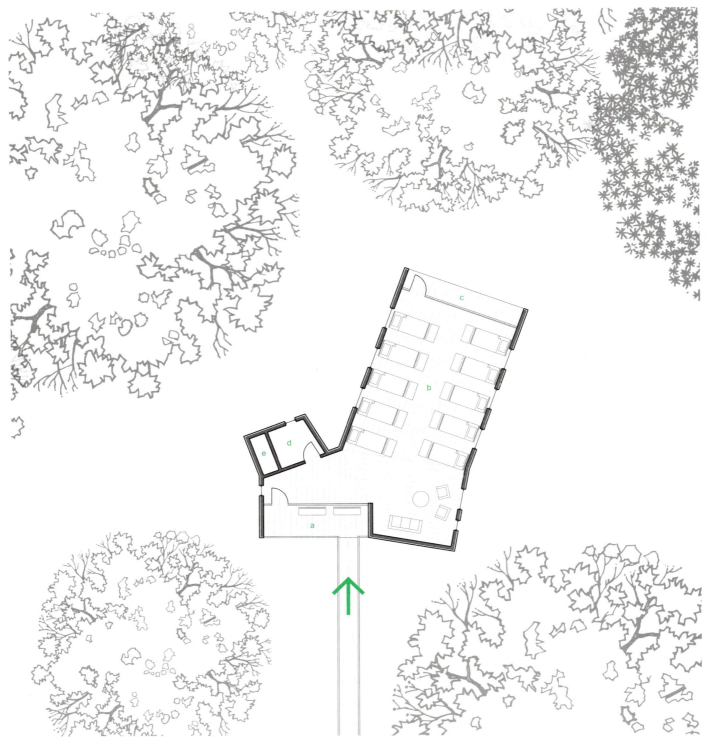

Each cabin provides an outdoor porch and balcony, interior social space, changing room, mechanical room, and sleeping area for ten campers.

Plan of Cabin Type 1A

a Porch
b Sleeping quarters
c Balcony
d Dressing room
e Mechanical room

218   Material—Detail

Material Assembly

Diagram

a Standing seam metal
b Waterproof underlay
c Roof cavity sheathing
d Roof cavity framing
e Roof sheathing
f Insulation
g Roof rafters
h Ceiling panels
i Engineered roof beam
j Roof vent
k Rainscreen panel
l Waterproofing
m Rainscreen framing
n Rainscreen sheathing
o Insulation
p Interior wall planking
q Interior wall framing
r Finished floor planking
s Laminated floor deck
t Floor joist
u Engineered floor beam
v Engineered wall column
w Air inlet screen
x Wood pier
y Welded steel base plate
z Reinforced concrete footing
aa Sheet metal gutter

J-Camp

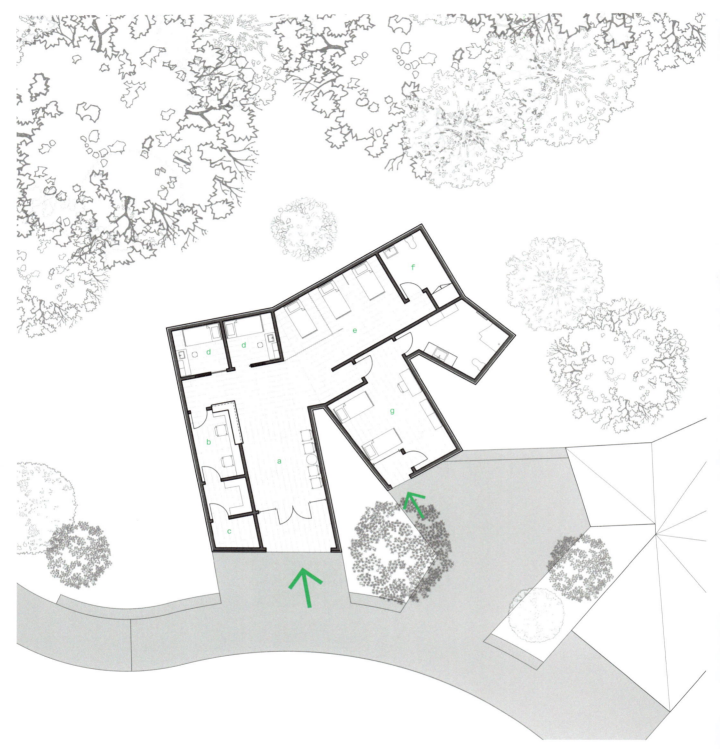

First Aid Floor Plan

a Entry and waiting
b Nurse station with medicine storage
c Mechanical room
d Private patient rooms
e Treatment area
f Bathroom
g Nurse private quarters

Material—Detail

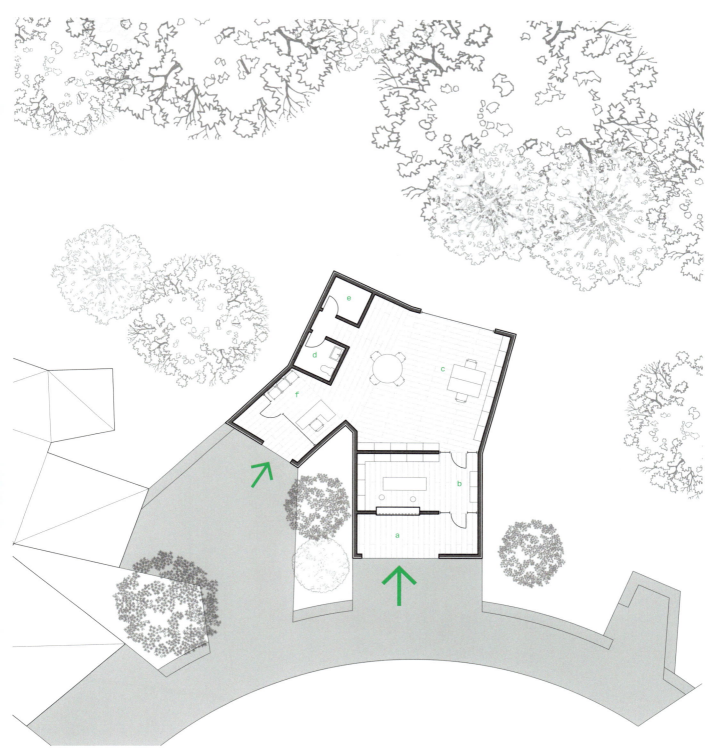

Canteen and Office
Floor Plan

a   Entry with sales counter
b   Shop display
c   Offices
d   Bathroom
e   Mechanical room
f   Camp information desk

J-Camp

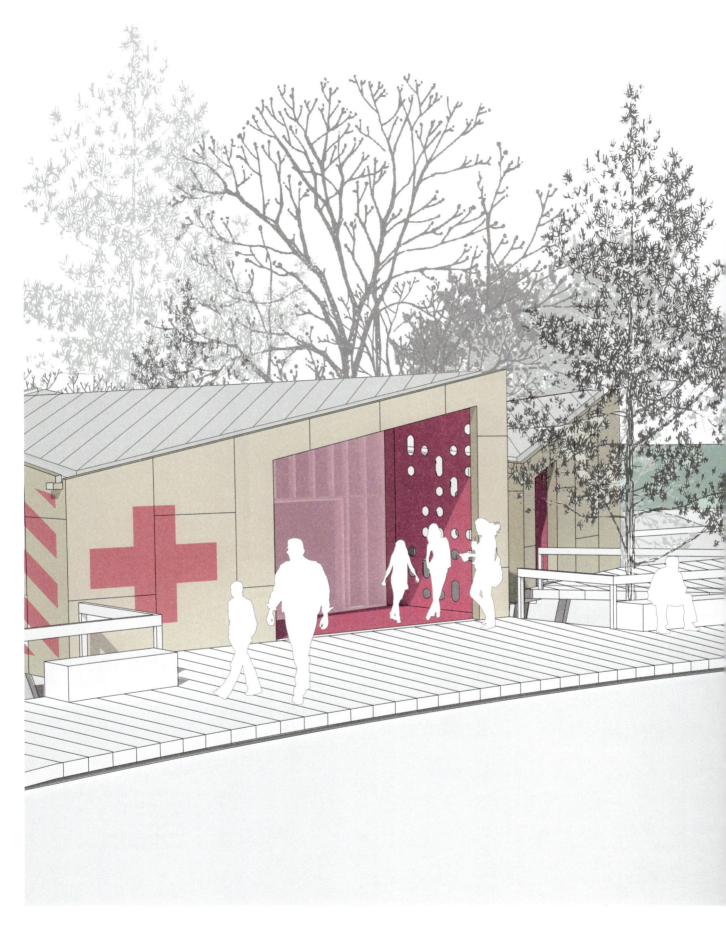

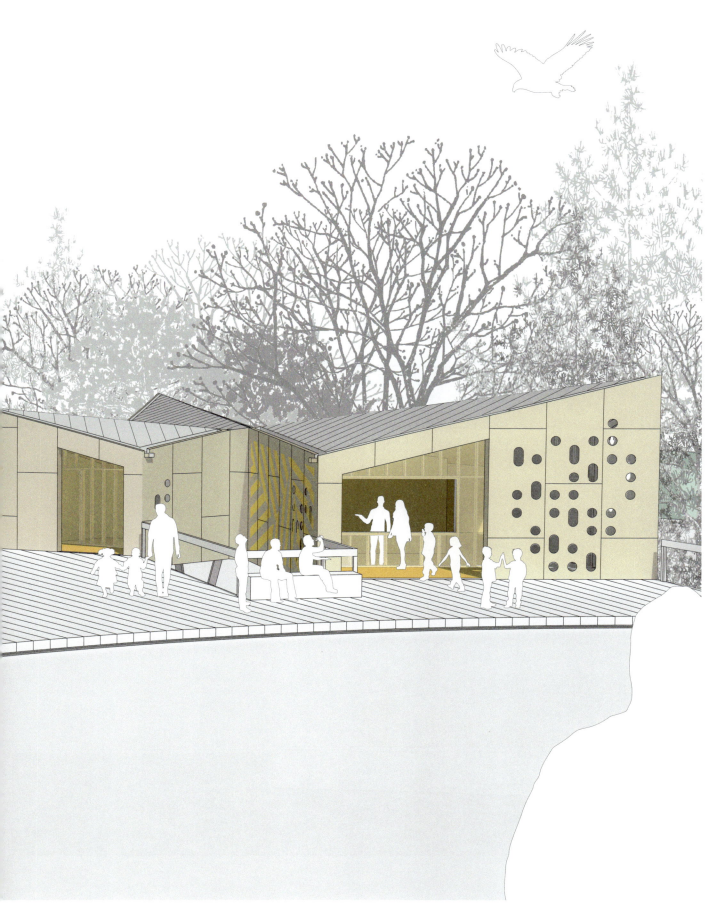

Canteen and Office
Elevation and Section

Material—Detail

First Aid
Elevation and Section

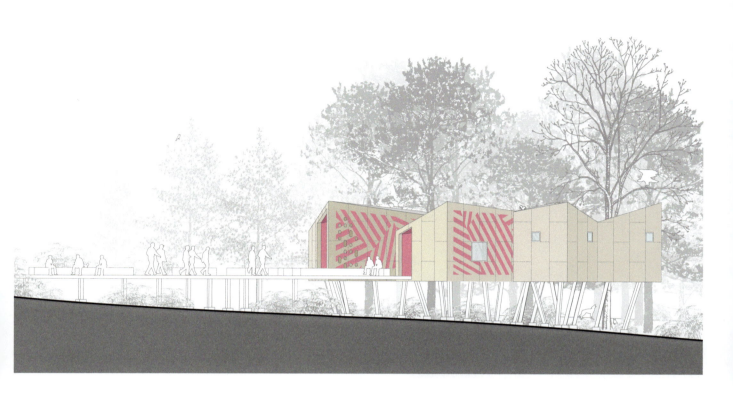

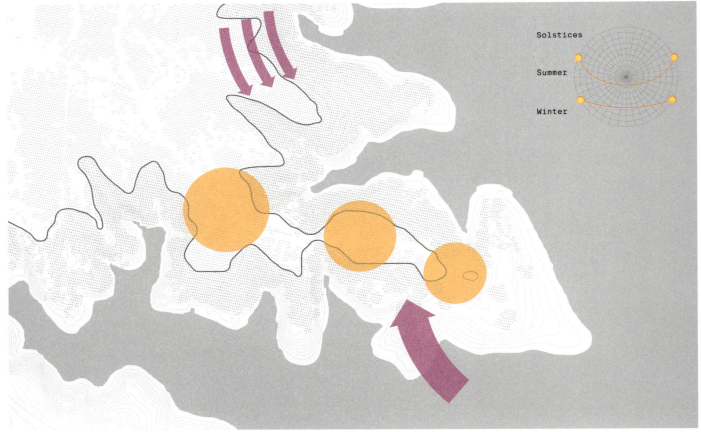

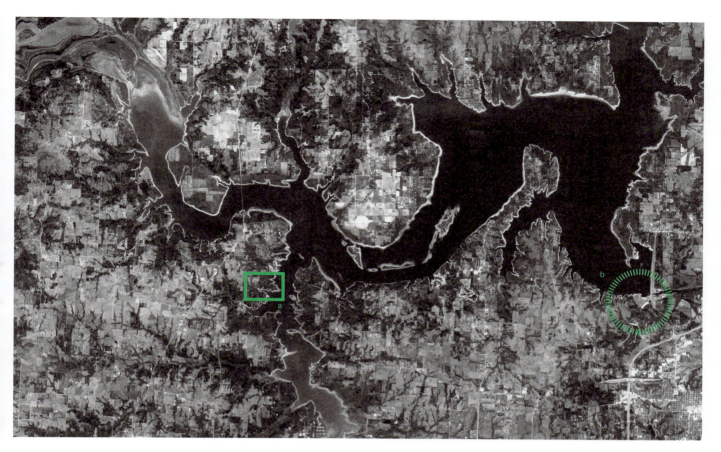

a   127-acre peninsula operated by the U.S. Army Corp of Engineers and under a twenty-year contract lease with J-Camp to develop a year-round campground site.

b   Completed in 1943, the Lake Texoma Dam is located on the Red River between Texas and Oklahoma. The damn facilitates flood control, water supply, and power production while providing water recreation areas managed by the U.S. Army Corp of Engineers.

Previous page: Detail image of site (above) and site study of prevailing winds, line of floodplain, canopy coverage, and possible sites for public commons.

J-Camp

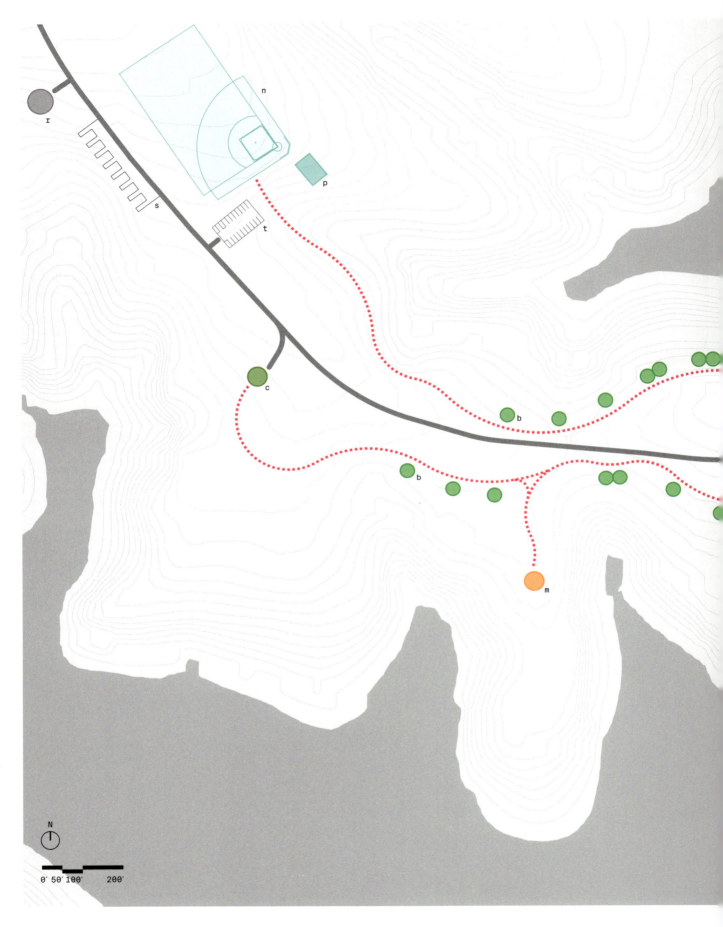

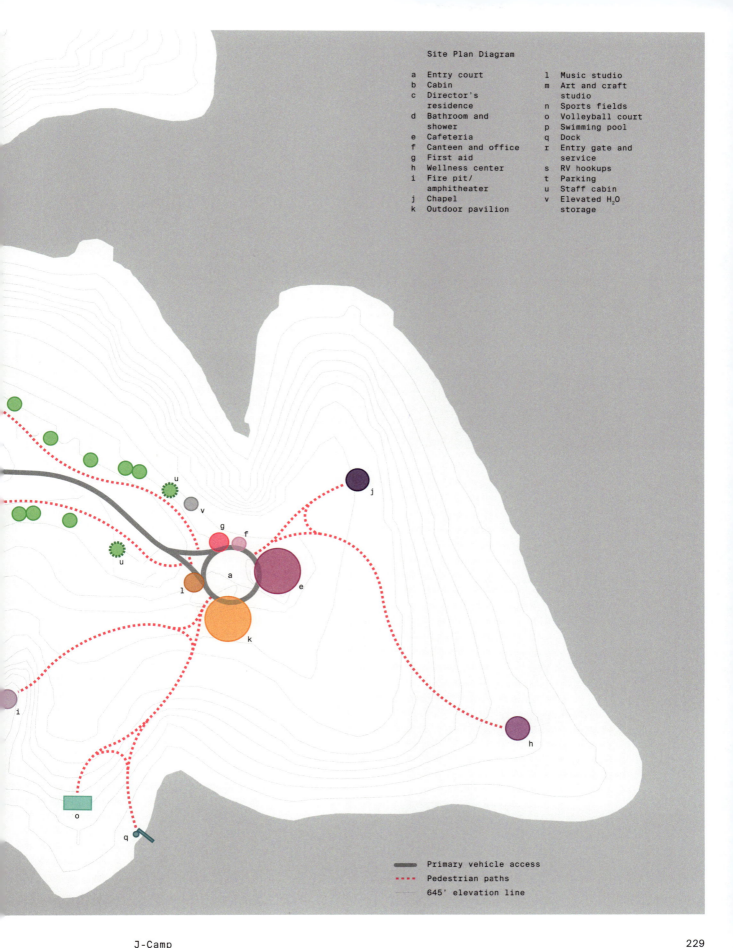

J-Camp

Cabin Type 1B
Elevation and Section

Cabin Type 2B
Elevation and Section

J-Camp

Cabin Type 1B Section Detail

232   Material—Detail

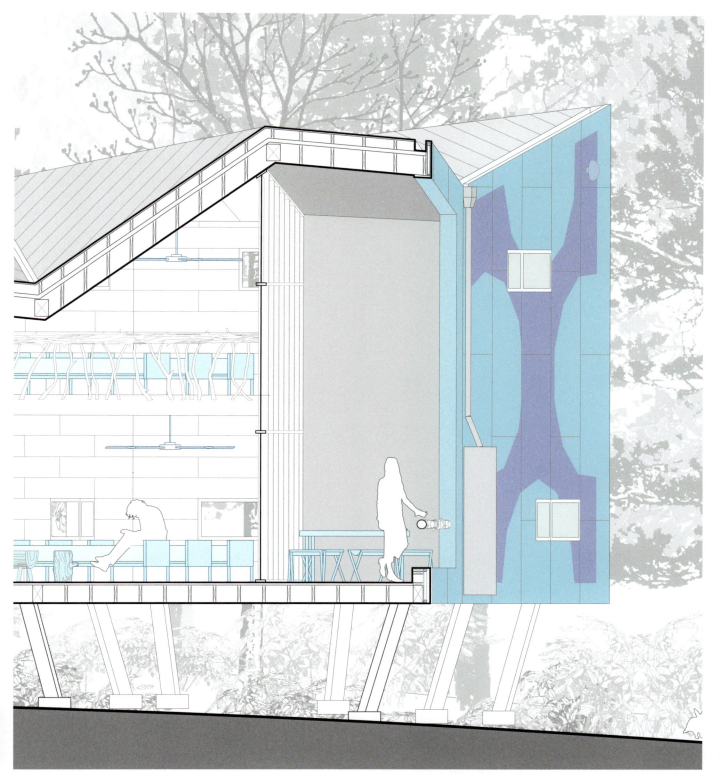

Cabin Type 2B Section Detail

J-Camp

233

Cafeteria Perspective
and Section

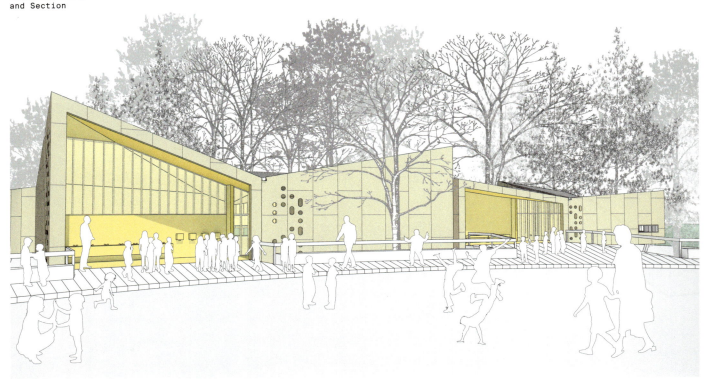

Cafeteria Floor Plan

a Entry vestibule
b Bathrooms
c Seating area and stage
d Servery
e Kitchen
f Dishwashing area
g Staff sleeping quarters
h Outdoor smoker cooking
i Porch
j Service entry

J-Camp

Outdoor Pavilion and
Recreation Center
Elevation and Section

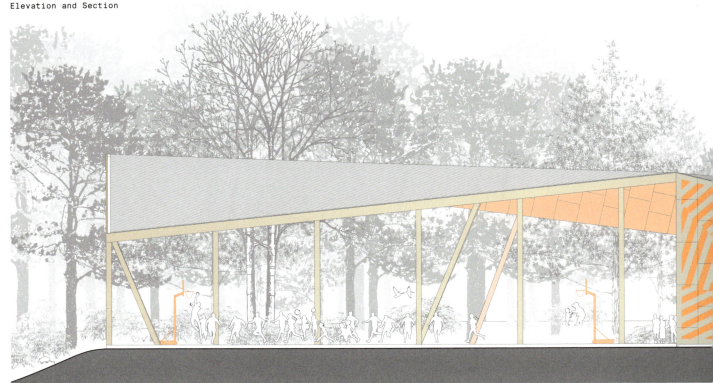

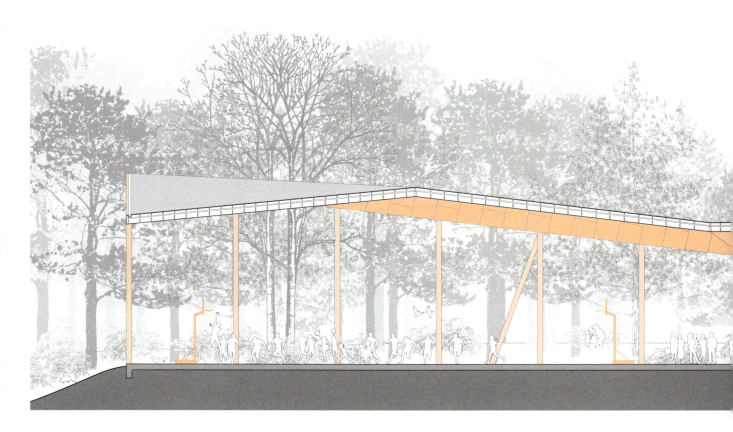

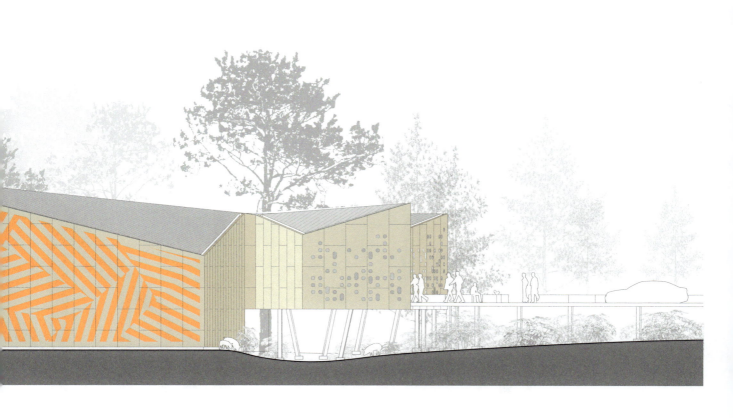

J-Camp

Inside Corner

Client	Vasquez & Pratt
Dates	2011-2014
Location	Houston, Texas

Tiny interior vestibules produce *inside corners* to conceal all doors and thresholds that lead from the shared public areas to private rooms.

Inside Corner is a private residence with an expansive interior and a series of distributed gardens where large family gatherings and cultural events are frequently hosted. The house's shared social spaces are open and continuous with one another, as well as visible through and accessible to a central exterior planted courtyard that provides an array of local herbs and edibles to one of the clients, a former restaurateur. The gardens are designed and maintained with indigenous plants and trees that generate a continually changing set of interior and exterior spaces.

Tiny interior vestibules produce *inside corners* to conceal all doors and thresholds that lead from shared public areas to private rooms. Private bedrooms are buffered from the central courtyard, separated by gallery corridors that allow artwork to be viewed across and through the courtyard space from the public areas.

The front and back porches are offset from one another, shifted toward opposite ends of the courtyard. These covered outdoor spaces allow diagonal views from the street to the lush central courtyard and through to the tree-lined backyard. The two porches, one for entry and one for dining, are almost identical in detailing. But subtle differences reflect their use and position. Each is framed by a custom steel and glass entry wall, enclosed on one side by large vertical stone slab panels and punctuated by a single steel column that supports the roof and frames an adjacent ornamental garden. The back dining porch integrates built-in cooking and serving areas. The front entrance is screened by a custom stainless steel pivot gate. Perforated stainless steel sheet was cut and bent to form long, structurally stable geometries that are mounted on the gate's painted steel structure.

A modest palette of materials was selected for the interior to highlight the clients' objects and unique furnishings. A bright-white terrazzo floor flecked with green marble chips defines the continuous shared spaces of the house, punctuated by strategically located pieces of built-in furniture that are accented with vibrant shades of green, yellow, and aqua paint.

Inside Corner

The west edge of the house faces a north-south boulevard that crosses over a freeway. A densely planted garden wall shelters the house's side garden from daily traffic and provides a lush backdrop to pedestrian life.

Inside Corner

1   The building footprint is
    shifted to form small private
    gardens at the front and back
    of the house.

2   Shared spaces are located in
    the center, surrounding a lush
    exterior courtyard. Terraces
    extend from these spaces to
    front and back exterior gardens.

3   Tiny interior vestibules (blue)
    produce inside corners to
    conceal all doors and thresholds
    that lead to private rooms.

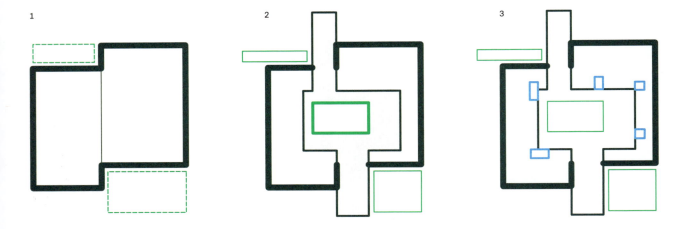

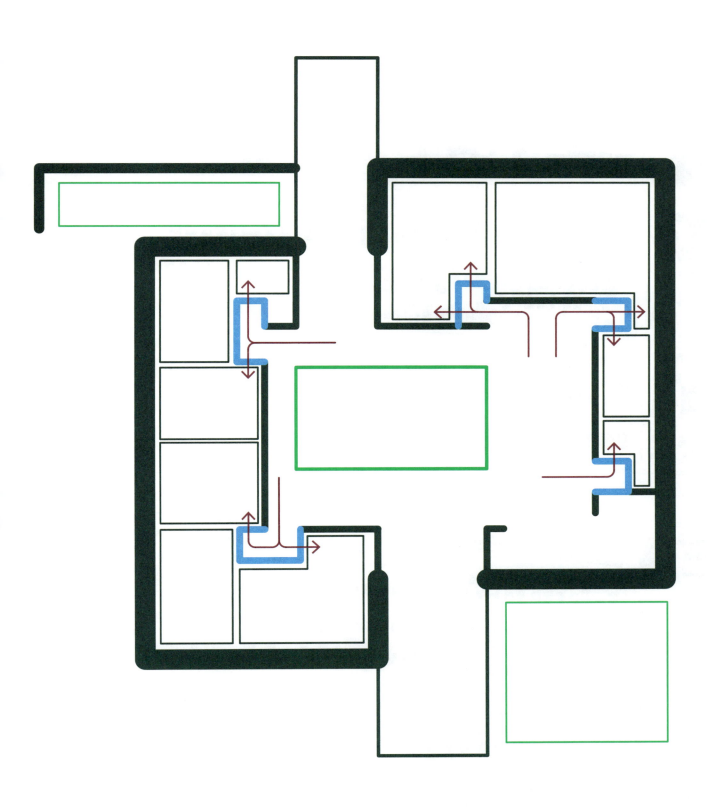

Inside Corner

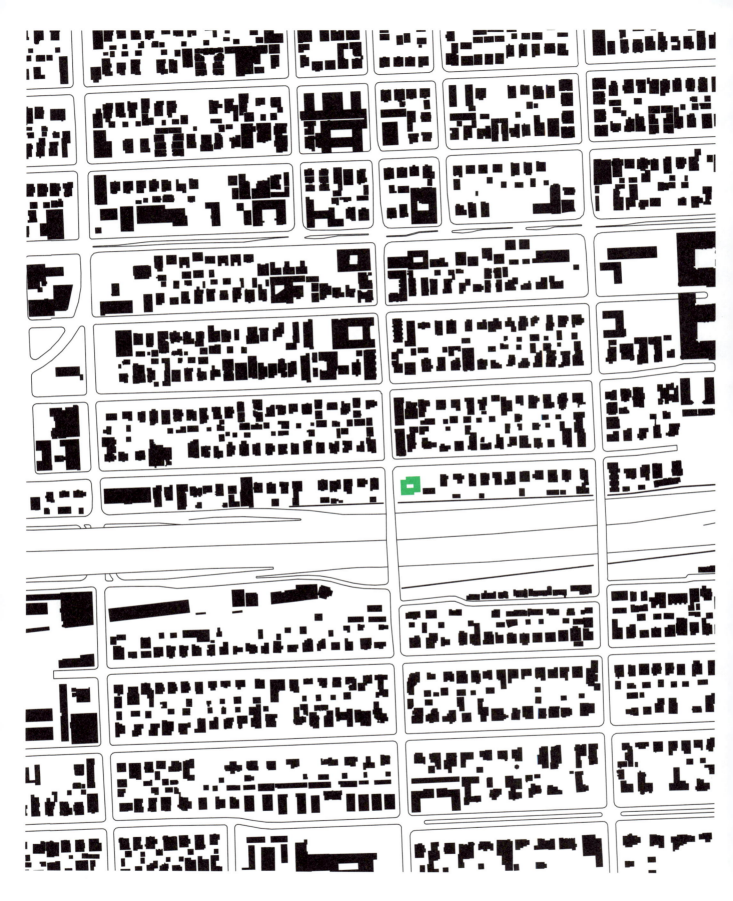

Material—Detail

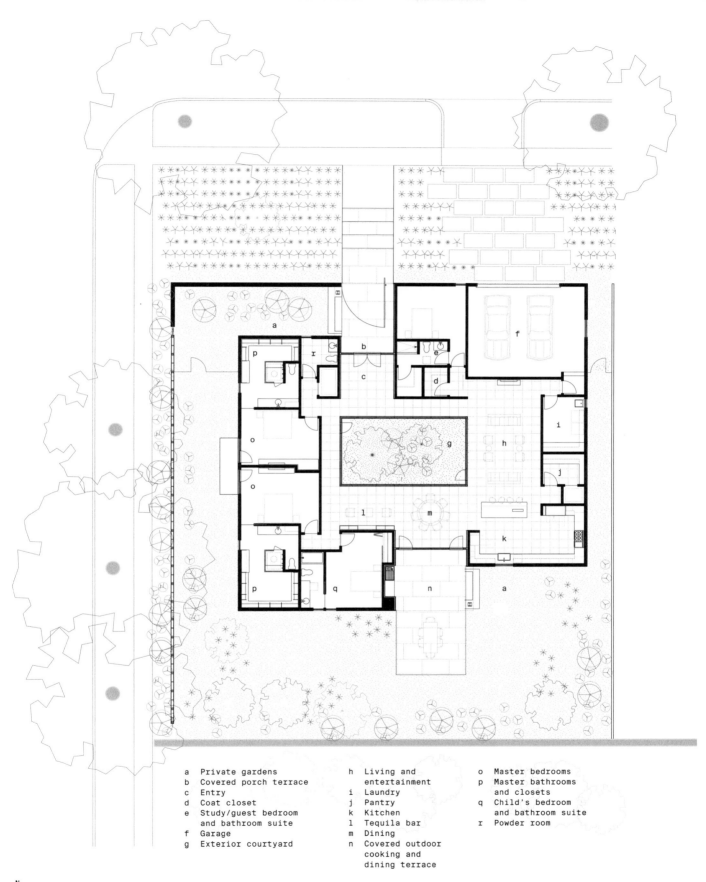

a Private gardens
b Covered porch terrace
c Entry
d Coat closet
e Study/guest bedroom and bathroom suite
f Garage
g Exterior courtyard
h Living and entertainment
i Laundry
j Pantry
k Kitchen
l Tequila bar
m Dining
n Covered outdoor cooking and dining terrace
o Master bedrooms
p Master bathrooms and closets
q Child's bedroom and bathroom suite
r Powder room

Inside Corner

247

Solar Shadow Studies

248　　　　Material—Detail

Section through Entry
and Courtyard

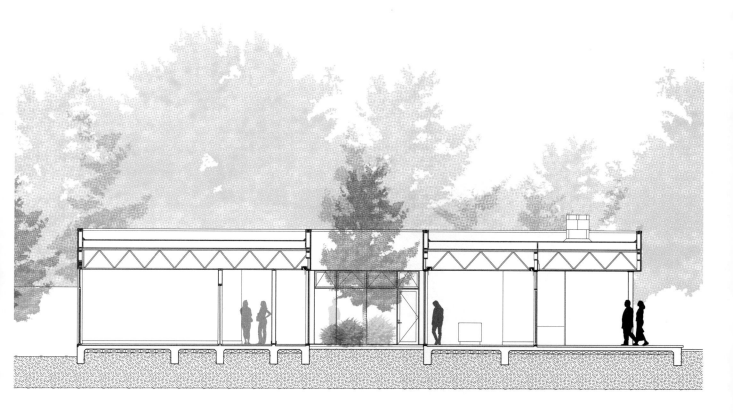

Inside Corner

Custom stainless steel entry gate

The gate pivots inward,
opening a large covered terrace
to the street.

Inside Corner 251

Interior views

Inside Corner

Notes No. 3

The recognition and understanding of systems is not automatic but requires selective, often subjective determination. The component parts that form a coherent system for one person may not add up to a system for another.

3.01 Graphic Systems

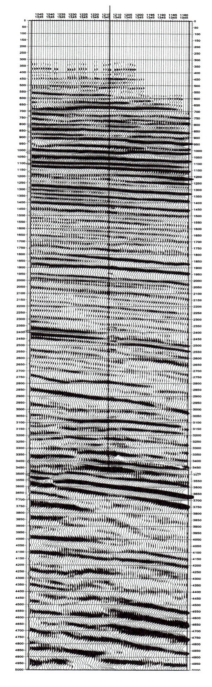

In design, pattern generally manifests in one of two distinct ways: as process (a model or instruction guide for the production of an object or system) or as representation (a repetitive motif or ornament). These two manifestations are not necessarily mutually exclusive and often are difficult to distinguish. Both perform, organize, and are critical in architecture.

In the Yoga Studio and Garden, the hardwood screen that wraps the building facade creates a pattern of small identical ipe members composed by a set of relational rules that register the density of the members with the uniformity of their distribution. The pieces aggregate to form a legible system that is both constructed and projected. Coincidentally, the design's dual performance and representation resonated with one client, a geologist in Houston who routinely evaluates natural gas exploration imaging, scanning and parsing these abstract, layered, two-dimensional patterns for their resource potential. Exploration imaging uses algorithms to graphically translate material relationships deep underground so as to identify pockets of natural gas.

3.02 Sequenced Practice

Referred to as a *shala*, the Yoga Studio building is designated for sharing the traditions of Ashtanga yoga practice taught by R. Sharath Jois of Mysore, India. Ashtanga yoga uses Sanskrit to numerically identify specific positions and transitions—sequences that build in quantity and difficulty as students progress. In a class, the Ashtanga instructor calls each *asana* (pose or posture) and counts each *vinyasa* (movement between poses) in Sanskrit. Students of varying levels practice independently in a collective space. Specific sequences of postures and transitions structure each student's daily practice.

Our design of a built-in cabinet of storage lockers in the *shala* includes a set of custom laser-etched Sanskrit key tags, intended to reinforce the learning of Ashtanga practice. Two sets of tags—one deep red, one green—allow for a periodic graphic update within the space.

3.03   Serial Details

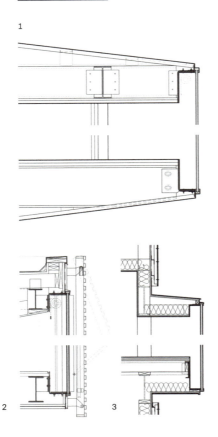

Architectural details are carried from project to project and tested iteratively through new scales and contexts. While similar in their assembly relationships, the details transform in each new context due to differences in material, finish, fasteners, application, siting, proportion, and environmental conditions. Serial details are often generated in facade systems, roof systems, lighting systems, surface treatments, built-in furniture, and architectural ornamental steel.

In this instance, a steel and glass facade system—which allows for the interior appearance of floor-to-ceiling glass with no mullions—uses a pocket detail to capture large butt-glazed insulated glass panels top and bottom, braced by flat vertical steel members, either painted bar stock or stainless. Constructed versions of the detail are found in Plug-on (1), Yoga Studio (2), and 9° House (3).

3.04   Operative Models

In addition to digital drawings and diagrams, physical models are critical to the study and development of most projects in our office. For the Yoga Studio, the haptic qualities of the hardwood screen were evaluated in numerous iterations, using paper and wood. A one-half-inch scale model of the final version of the screen was carefully constructed and held stable by an abstracted floor plate and wall assembly. A peephole drilled in the back allowed a glimpse into an approximation of the interior practice space, leading to last-minute feedback and adjustments to the screen's pattern design.

3.05   YS2

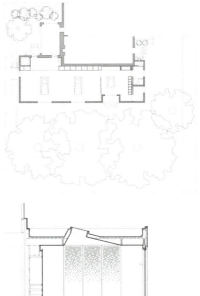

256   Material—Detail

YS2 is a second private yoga studio developed on a registered historic property in Houston. The project negotiates the renovation of a modern 1960s addition to a historic, two-story brick residence built in 1919. While city officials initially demanded that the 1960s addition be demolished and the house be restored to its original condition, our office advocated and petitioned for the significance of this modern add-on, noting that it was one of eight additions built within the same era to house design-related home offices on the same historic city block.

A set of vibrant, tactile elements were fabricated and strategically placed within the otherwise open and light-filled space. The colors and material textures encourage students to engage the architectural elements, including lockers, privacy screen, stone bench, and aluminum shoe rack. Deep cabinet drawers for storage of yoga mats are ventilated in a grid pattern. Articulated ceiling openings and skylights allow diffuse light within the practice space.

3.06 Carryover

In both yoga studios, we designed similar white built-in cabinets that organize the space, dividing the primary practice area from the bathroom and dressing areas. Both cabinets are detailed to appear neither completely built-in nor independent (freestanding) but as exerting an ambiguous importance within the space.

In the Yoga Studio, a custom white-lacquered built-in cabinet divides and organizes the second level into two zones, an open studio space and a slim bathroom. Incorporated into the cabinet interior are drawers, a Murphy bed and desk, seating, and storage—all of which face the studio. On the opposite side, sliding glass doors and compact bathroom fixtures face the shower and dressing area. The cabinet's bright white exterior contrasts with a glossy, deep-red interior paint, a surprising aspect when the cabinet doors are first opened.

In YS2, a similarly detailed built-in cabinet separates the main practice space from a shower room and separate toilet room. The cabinet organizes thirty daily-use lockers in which students can store personal belongings. The bright white interior contrasts with the vibrant pixilation of three saturated colors within the locker interiors: brick red, vibrant red, and grape.

3.07 Material Limits

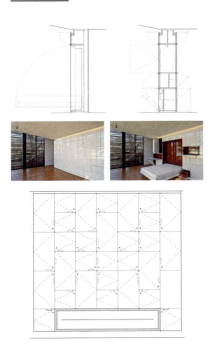 

Oak Forest Pool House is a modest public building that includes changing rooms, an office, and mechanical support for an inner-city pool in Houston. The aim was to create a graphically distinct, welcoming public amenity that met the client's requirements for function, budget, security, and maintenance.

Using cast-in-place concrete allowed for two buildings with bold formal and graphic roof elements to be constructed using a limited number of trades on-site. The concrete surfaces express the rough imprint of the board forms—presenting architectural details that convey a low-tech labor process and craft.

Cast with circular and semicircular openings, the butterfly roofs cantilever independently above a threshold space between the buildings, providing dappled natural light at the exterior entry passage to the public pool.

3.08   A Given Bungalow

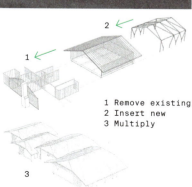

1 Remove existing
2 Insert new
3 Multiply

The Menil Collection in Houston invited our office to participate in a competition to plan the renovation of and design an addition for one of its existing gray bungalows, in which a new restaurant and bar was to be housed. The bungalows represent a collection of domestic and commercial programs that both define and support one of the most compelling public neighborhoods in the city. The Menil building depends on the visual consistency and scale of this repetitive, organizational fabric to position itself as an exception within the aesthetic context. Our approach to reimagining the given bungalow was first to preserve its outward form, scale, and materiality and, second, to expand its interior to accommodate a more collective, institutional space.

Interior partitions were removed and replaced with a delicate painted steel lattice insert that supported and exposed a dramatic interior volume, shifting the emphasis from small, cellular domestic spaces to a single public volume. The bungalow and steel lattice structure were then repeated to create a collection of connected buildings to accommodate dining, kitchen services, and support. Varied in size and proportion, the buildings were staggered along a new public access—maintaining the appearance of a collection of small, domestic buildings. Our office was not selected for the project, but the built design clearly (and curiously) reflects our proposed site organization, addition, and plan.

3.09   Conservation, Engagement, Research

258   Material—Detail

The garden in Hempstead, Texas, represents an uncommon but increasingly important type: a landscape that supports both preservation and public engagement. The garden contains a diverse array of plant species from the Texas-Mexico border regions, many of which have disappeared from their natural habitat or are under threat from the pressures of human development. The center we were commissioned to design would allow this mission to be expanded to include more experimental plant research and seed propagation and a focus on regional environmental concerns.

3.10   Cycles

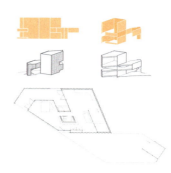

A large retention pond on the Hempstead property is used to mitigate flooding and to harvest rainwater. Our design proposal for the research center distributed watershed and retention basins across the landscape to integrate with phased planting initiatives and walking paths. In addition, the proposed building provided multiple rainwater collection points on the roof and a low-tech irrigation system to support all ornamental and research gardens within the building footprint.

An aerial view of one of Houston's flooded highways demonstrates the fallout from years of private development that neglected to account for the prolonged material consequences of building within marshlands and critical watershed zones, disrupting the coordinated water flow of the city's four major bayous.

3.11   Material Transfer, Application

Sheet pile is an industrial weathered-steel product designed to retain both earth and water for a variety of construction site types. The long, heavy-gauge interlocking panels are driven vertically into the ground to form a corrugated surface of raw, weathered steel. Their application may be temporary—to stage ground excavation during construction—or permanent: to prevent flooding, stabilize underground structures, and protect foundations from groundwater damage. We imagined a new application and aesthetic for sheet pile panels in the design of domestic architecture: a single-family house sited within the 100-year floodplain on White Oak Bayou in Houston.

Properties such as this are threatened by infrequent but inevitable dramatic flooding—a common issue in the city, where flood maps are being redrawn to reflect the environmental devastation of the past ten years.

The sheet pile house prototype designates a large, open-sided, covered space at the ground level, allowing outdoor gardens and grounds to extend through the house while anticipating periodic flooding. The ground and the structural slab direct the flow of water toward a retention basin at the rear yard, while the sheet pile panels prevent water flow from infiltrating slightly elevated storage, work, and service spaces.

3.12   Material Transfer, Value

Notes No. 3

Materials do not exist independent of systems of bias and external reference that color how those materials are seen and valued. A simple handmade bag, constructed with printed paper, demonstrates a dramatic transfer of material value under dynamic political and economic conditions in the late twentieth century. The paper used for the bag is actually Cambodian currency that was abolished under the reign of Pol Pot and his army of Khmer Rouge communists from 1975 to 1979. Domestic trade and commerce during those years were legal only in the form of barter. Currency thus lost its original, socially constructed value as money and came to instead be valued for its performance and aesthetics alone; that is, for being a lightweight, pliable paper with a printed pattern.

3.13   Janelia Farm Housing

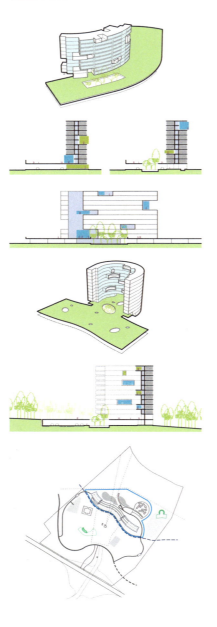

Our work on large institutional building and planning strategies includes the Janelia Farm Research Campus. Located on a 689-acre property in Loudoun County, Virginia, Janelia is a scientific research center operated by the Howard Hughes Medical Institute (HHMI). The existing campus contains a research laboratory (designed by architect Rafael Viñoly), conference housing, visitor housing, and a preservation easement and large conservation easement on the bank of the Potomac River. The campus includes HHMI's neuroscience research labs, which compete globally for top postdocs, fellows, and scientific staff.

Our office was commissioned to develop a site, building, and program study for sixty units of new housing on the campus. Four potential sites were studied, and a unique organizational strategy was developed for each. Critical to the study was a demonstration of how each site scheme would shape the communal role of housing on the Janelia campus. Quality long-term housing supports the rigorous work style of the scientists (many of whom live on campus with their families) and will serve as a recruiting tool to counter the traditional tenure-track trajectory for young scientists. Tower and Horseshoe were design proposals that examined the potentials of a mid-rise building with a large public terrace at its base and distributed social spaces on the upper levels.

3.14   Janelia Type Models

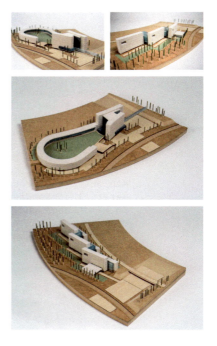

In choosing to research with HHMI at the Janelia campus, postdocs reject the tenure-track system of most research universities. In return for giving up the security

260   Material—Detail

of tenure, HHMI's researchers are provided with full funding for their research, freeing them from the time-consuming grant-application process. To support this unique research model, HHMI sought to provide campus housing for postdocs and their families in the hope of building a robust social community through shared infrastructure.

    Lasso and Zig-Zag are two of the six organizational models developed to demonstrate the lifestyle potential of the campus. The models, which balance domestic privacy with communal and collective spaces, allowed the client to understand architecture's agency and provided clear, comparative terms for use in evaluation and selection. Zig-Zag was ultimately chosen. However, the final stages of design development coincided with the 2008 market crash in the United States, leading HHMI to hire a local design-build contractor to complete the project.

3.15   Graphic Surface

The term *supergraphics* describes a body of work that emerged in the 1960s that applied large-scale two-dimensional graphics to existing architectural spaces with paint. While contemporary use of the term more generally refers to large numbers, words, or images applied to building surfaces, early applications of these two-dimensional graphics were intended to destabilize, transform, or negate existing architectural form. Early supergraphics register and make legible the tension and coincidence between two-dimensional surfaces and the three-dimensional forms they cover. Our work often uses this concept as a point of departure and inspiration.

3.16   Pliable

Pliable is a body of academic research that references supergraphics to explore and amplify the multiple, simultaneous readings of surface and form in architecture. The experimental research—conducted through studios and seminars at Rice School of Architecture and led by Dawn Finley—uses textiles and synthetic, pliable, sheet-based materials to foreground the fabrication of medium and large architectural objects. Sheet-based constructions allow surface and form (which are materially separate in supergraphics) to be congruent, while providing new opportunities for representation, organization, and structure.

    Textile processes almost exclusively use flat patterns and surfaces to generate form, and the translation from two to three dimensions occurs with little mediation. Advanced digital modeling software is surprisingly ineffective at simulating the structural and aesthetic effects of sheet-based materials; therefore, students engage in full-scale fabrication and prototyping. The architectural objects assert the two-dimensional (textile) graphic surface as an active, critical organizing element in the development of form. Each object foregrounds the pliable relationship between surface and form, exploiting surface as an operative design element.

3.17   Radial Wrap

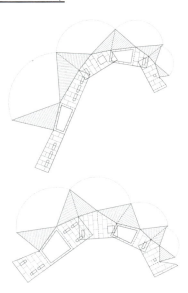

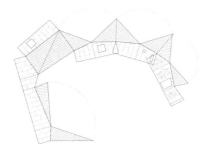

In the garment and other textile-based industries, patterns are instructional drawings that describe flat, two-dimensional shapes that are typically cut out of pliable, sheet-based material and then assembled (stitched together) to make a three-dimensional form. Our work often borrows drawing techniques and conventions from the textile industry, modified to an appropriate scale and level of complexity as a method of foregrounding the architectural surface. Drawings are never neutral instruments of pure documentation. In addition to biasing the registration and position of an architectural work, drawings have the potential to amplify and align with the conceptual framework of a project.

These three unwrapped surface drawings of two camp cabins and a canteen building demonstrate the scalar and organizational variation in the J-Camp building system—a system that was originally conceived of in plan. As the system materialized and building types developed in detail, the focus shifted to the three-dimensional relationships between exterior wall and roof surfaces. While the floor elevation remains flat, the coincident vertices of each roof and wall surface are elevated or lowered together to modulate spatial proportion, orientation, views, ventilation, and water flow off the building.

Initially a representational exercise, studying the building enclosures as unwrapped, flattened skins generated a series of new building variations derived through the drawing technique and its formal, geometric rules.

3.18   Profile, Pattern, Graphic

When viewed in isolation, each of the J-Camp building surfaces is a simple quadrilateral, flat at the base and vertical edges, while canted at the top. The overall width of each building is an increment of the rainscreen panels, which are mounted vertically in a running-bond pattern. Large, bold graphic patterns are superimposed onto each discrete face, inset from the edges and discontinuous with the building skin wrapper. The application of these painted graphics is indifferent to the cement fiber rainscreen panel joints.

3.19   Dazzle

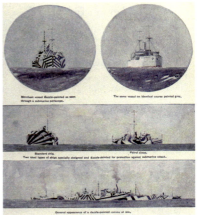

(Visually) disruptive patterning was proposed in 1917 by Norman Wilkinson, a naval lieutenant and painter, to protect the British Navy from German submarines. Ships could not be made invisible through regular camouflage because of the constantly changing light and weather conditions at sea, but by painting them with strong patterns their recognizable shapes could be rendered as apparently distinct masses. Dazzle painting made it difficult for a U-boat to determine the exact position or direction of the ship it wished to attack. The patterns were designed for maximum distortion when viewed using a periscope.

—*Encyclopædia Britannica*, 1922

The application of razzle-dazzle patterning on the public commons buildings of J-Camp references this distortion technique, using vibrant pink, orange, and yellow. When water levels rise due to periodic flooding, the buildings appear to float on the lake as novel nautical objects in the wooded landscape.

3.20 Julia's

Several years before the opening of Houston's first light-rail line, connecting the medical center to downtown, we worked with a client to invigorate this critical urban corridor. The site was an existing, one-story, derelict corner building in Midtown. The entire building was gutted, including required exterior demolition and structuring of two glass facades, with full replacement of all building systems, and redesigned to house a restaurant with full kitchen and bar. After the installation of the rail line, Julia's was one of the first local commercial destinations to open along Main Street; its vibrant interior served as an early landmark along the somewhat vacant light-rail corridor. The interior walls were treated with a cosmetic-inspired abstract graphic (rouge, plum, fuchsia, and espresso blocks) that wrapped the walls and ceilings, indifferent to alignment with the interior. The floor was coated with a ruby-gloss epoxy compound, matching the color of the menu, which highlights authentic Mexican fare. Our office designed the space, architectural built-ins, graphics, and signage, carefully calibrating scalar details to form a loose collection of distinct urban graphic components.

3.21 Color Performance

Our interest in and use of colors stems not from cultural references or assumed meanings but from their visual, experiential, and technical effects. At least one scientific study has found that plant growth can be affected by the color of a plant's environment. Reflected light from adjacent plants and the surrounding environment plays a role in how plants respond and survive (growing taller, growing sturdier, bearing more fruit, etc.). In this image, researchers use plastic mulch and textiles that reflect specific colors onto tomato plants. The study attempted to quantify the effects of color on the growth rate, size, taste, and color of tomatoes and speculates on which environmental conditions the color reflection simulates. Color is recognized as a potential tool by which agricultural producers might noninvasively alter plant species.

3.22 Wasabi Wrap

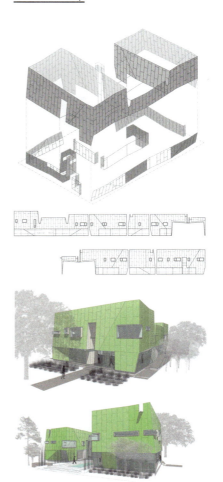

This private residence was designed for a multigenerational family in Houston. At the center of the site is a private garden, pool, and terrace that serve as a spatial buffer for two distinct households within. The two-story house is structured as one large and one small volume—each containing sleeping, bathing, dining, and lounging areas—linked by a central double-height kitchen that opens directly to the terrace and pool. The outer facade of the house is designed to screen the interior spaces from the outside, while providing specific views from the interior spaces to a series of perimeter gardens. Facets, cuts, creases, and perforations are some of the techniques used to articulate the outer enclosure as a continuous wrapper that links the discrete volumes of the house.

The exterior material is a vibrant rainscreen cladding made of factory-cut fiber cement panels with integral color—wasabi green—a graphic departure from the adjacent brick and stucco residences. Sited on a boulevard with old-growth oak trees and densely packed ornamental gardens, the house is intended to reflect a modest green tint on the surrounding landscapes, subtly altering the visual context (and possibly the area's ecology).

3.23 White Oak Bayou Studio

The courtyard house typology has a long, global history, extending to well before the minimal productions of modernism. Our interest in the courtyard house stems from its material correspondence to organization—situating a thick outer edge of domestic activity and an open center that visually and spatially connects a series of discrete rooms. The outer surface is often heavy or opaque with minimal openings to the urban context, while the inner surface is light and transparent.

This private studio and residence was commissioned by a well-regarded local artist to house a workspace, an exhibition space, and a modest dwelling. Rather than formally separate these demands, the art studio and domestic spaces are connected through a glazed exterior courtyard that sits directly in the center of the building. With glass on all sides, the courtyard appears to be a discrete object that connects the distinct, acoustically separated program elements. The courtyard, which contains a pool, is used as a short-cut between spaces, allowing work and leisure to overlap in Houston's temperate climate throughout the year. Custom perforated weathered-steel sliding panels allow the residence and studio to be completely open to the front street or closed down in the evening like a compound. Inside Corner references this design, including its courtyard typology and kinetic, screened facade, while translating its programmatic and material conditions to a dense, more urban context.

3.24 Compound

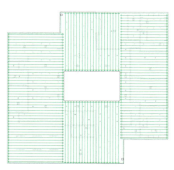

RCP with Engineered Truss Layout

Finca Nogales is a commissioned residential compound consisting of private domestic residences, service outpost buildings (kitchen, laundry), and shared public amenities (dining, study, social meetings) organized around a series of gardens and orchards on a 22,000-acre cattle ranch in northern Argentina, near Salta. The private compound houses a barn, seed house, and residence for a ranch foreman with adjoining stables and horse-riding pen. In addition to the working cattle ranch, Finca Nogales opens seasonally to international travelers for retreats and other events.

The site and building design first impose a long, thick wall, creating an edge and boundary to the harsh, wild surroundings. Adjacent and attached to the interior surface of the wall are a series of discrete one- and two-story buildings, each with unique private gardens and outdoor spaces. Two buildings for collective activity break from the edge to form an open social center on the property. This center serves as a focal point for all residents, staff, and guests. The buildings are constructed of locally sourced materials using local labor and labor practices to produce a formally modest, materially complex set of buildings that define one edge of the property.

3.25   Legible Systems

Inside Corner uses two-by-six wood framing coordinated with premanufactured wood roof trusses that are oriented perpendicular to the outer edge of the central courtyard. The house is based upon a grid that enables the systematic coordination of wood framing, windows, floor joints, cabinets, glazing of the courtyard, lighting, plumbing, and services. All interior and exterior wall framing members are spaced sixteen inches on center, and all other systems are based on multiples of sixteen.

Engineered for maximum efficiency, flat, manufactured residential trusses are located and spaced relative to structural forces, and thus are out of synch with the adjoining wall-framing pattern. As a result, the services, lighting, skylights, and openings in the ceiling are often out of synch with the cavity spacing and structural lines of the wall system. When the smaller finishing elements of a residence are installed, the efficiency in one trade produces waste and complexity in others. We opted for a less efficient truss spacing, requiring the purchase of additional trusses to gain the three-dimensional coherence and coordination expected of a building. The patterns of building systems are spatial, organizational, and legible.

3.26   Detailed Expression

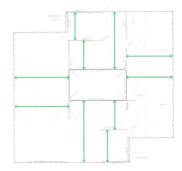

Engineered Truss Diagram

When viewed from a distance, the courtyard enclosure of Inside Corner appears to be a bold graphic object, occupying the center of a continuous, undifferentiated space. When viewed up close, perpendicular to the glass surface, the enclosure recedes, giving way to the layered spaces of the house while providing spatial separation and distinction. This dual reading of object and surface (or looking at and looking through) is made deliberate by the architectural detailing—enabled and amplified by the black steel frames that cohere from a distance and serve as a repetitive background up close.

3.27   Double Boundary-Object

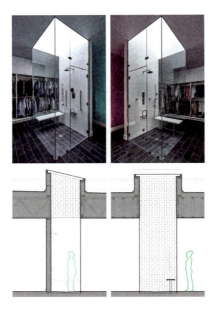

Inside Corner is designed with two almost identical master bathrooms, mirrored in plan and differentiated by wall color. A tall, slender glass shower enclosure punctuates the center of each space, serving as a spatial boundary between the closet dressing area and the vanity, sink, and toilet area. Not unlike the courtyard within the main part of the house, the glass shower allows for visibility across and through, making each space more expansive while also providing an architectural focal point. The shower enclosure is topped with a large glass skylight that is detailed to appear frameless and open to the sky. This dramatic punctuation of natural light further accentuates the visual presence of the glass enclosure as an object in the room.

3.28   Folded Sheet

A set of custom-fabricated, brake-form components punctuate the exterior facade of the Inside Corner house. The formal articulation of a side awning is derived from repetitive folds that crease six large stainless steel panels. The folds provide structural rigidity and ornament, while directing water flow away from an outdoor porch space below. Standing seams are capped with plate fasteners that link the panels and allow them to be tensioned back to the building facade. We developed adaptable details of assembly (e.g., the angle and location of folds, the location of drill holes) that were deployed serially to enable both horizontal and vertical mounting of panels, depending upon the functional application.

266   Material—Detail

3.29 Structural Skin

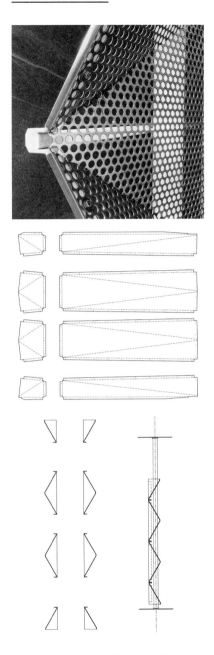

The front entrance of Inside Corner is screened by a custom stainless steel gate, one of several specialty architectural components. Perforated stainless steel sheet material is cut and bent to form long, structurally stable geometries that are mounted on an eighteen-inch-deep painted steel structure. The large, elegant, panelized skin hovers two inches off the ground and cantilevers almost ten feet. To open, the gate pivots inward from a six-inch pipe column, exposing a large covered terrace to the street. The gate combines custom-treated stainless steel sheet with more conventional off-the-shelf materials.

Notes No. 3

Credits

Project Credits

9° House
Dawn Finley, Mark Wamble, Jennifer Chen,
Eric Hughes, Andrew McFarland

Symonds(+) Teaching Laboratories
Dawn Finley, Mark Wamble, Jennifer Chen,
Duncan Davidson, Eric Hughes

Open Transfer
Dawn Finley, Mark Wamble, Matthew Austin,
Sam Brisendine, Mary Casper, Eric Hughes,
Jack Mussett

48' House
Dawn Finley, Mark Wamble

Klip
Dawn Finley, Mark Wamble, Blaine Brownell,
Wyatt Frantom, Pete Koehler, Ana Miljacki,
James Spearman

E-X-I-T
Dawn Finley, Mark Wamble, Jeanie Cravens,
Eric Hughes, Jack Mussett, Gray Peterson,
with collaborator Sam Youdal

Tending,(blue)
Dawn Finley, Mark Wamble, Ben Thorne,
with artist James Turrell

Yoga Studio and Garden
Dawn Finley, Mark Wamble, Jennifer Chen,
Kyle Henricks, Eric Hughes, Mark Watabe

Hempstead Research Center
Dawn Finley, Mark Wamble, Jennifer Chen,
Will Garris, Marissa Hebert, Eric Hughes

J-Camp
Dawn Finley, Mark Wamble, Patrick
Dario, Michael Kapinus, Michael Matthews,
Zachary Morrison

Inside Corner
Dawn Finley, Mark Wamble, Kyle Henricks,
Peter Muessig, Jack Mussett, Erin Ruhl

Office Credits, 1996-2021

Joseph Altschuler, Ken Andrews, Matthew
Austin, Sam Brisendine, Blaine Brownell,
Mary Casper, Jennifer Chen, Jeanie Cravens,
Patrick Dario, Duncan Davidson, Wyatt
Frantom, Will Garris, Marissa Hebert, Kyle
Henricks, Eric Hughes, Michael Kapinus,
Emily Kirkland, Pete Koehler, Michael
Matthews, Andrew McFarland, Ana Miljacki,
Zachary Morrison, Peter Muessig, Jack
Mussett, Gray Peterson, Erin Ruhl, Varia
Smirnova, James Spearman, Todd VanVarick,
Mark Watabe

Acknowledgments

Thank you to all of our past and present
clients, collaborators, colleagues,
and fabricators—including Musci Baglietto,
Michael Bell, Luke Bulman, John J.
Casbarian, Erik Hardenbol, Vel Hawes, Kyle
Henricks, Jenny and Mark Johnson, Lars
Lerup, Andrew McFarland, Ana Miljacki, Jack
Mussett, Steve Nash, Andrea Nasher, Ray
Nasher, Rachel Nystrom, Craig Pratt, Robert
E. Somol, Brett Terpeluk, Ben Thorne,
Carmen Vasquez, and Sam Youdal—for their
creative engagement with, support of,
and intellectual contributions to our practice over the years. Special thanks to
Reto Geiser for his friendship and critical
support in the development of this book;
to Scott Colman for his writings and
insights about our work; and to Renata Graw
for her precision and design expertise.

This book is dedicated to Leroy and Lucille,
who fill our world with energy, inspiration, and laughter; to my parents, Rosemary
and Earl Finley, and to the memory of
Mark's parents, Agnes and Glenn Wamble.

Image Credits

All drawings are the work of Interloop—Architecture and are courtesy and copyright © Interloop—Architecture. Unless otherwise noted, all other images are courtesy and copyright © Interloop—Architecture.

Part 1

9° House
© Benjamin Hill Photography
(pp. 16-17, 20-23, 28, 29 right, 30, 34-37)
© IA (pp. 25, 29 left)

Symonds (+) Teaching Laboratories
© Hester+Hardaway

Notes No. 1

1.02 Photographer unknown

1.02 New York Stock Exchange, New York, New York, 1977. Photo by Brownie Harris/Corbis, Getty Images

1.11 © ARCH+ 136

1.12 © Hester+Hardaway
News from Fondren [Rice University] 6, no. 2 (Winter 1997)

1.13 "How to Build Scenarios," in "Scenarios: The Future of the Future," special edition, *Wired Magazine*, January 1, 1995

1.14 © Hester+Hardaway
Design architect Mark Wamble with the office Bricker+Cannady

1.23 From KesselsKramer

1.25 Artist Boris Bally, www.borisbally .com. Photographer J.W. Johnson

1.25 Artist Rosalie Gascoigne. Photographer Ben Gascoigne

1.26 Christopher Alexander, "A City Is Not a Tree," *Architectural Forum* 122, no. 1 (April 1965)

1.27 Paul Rand, 1968 poster design for American Institute for Graphic Artists

1.27 Paul Rand, 1970 annual report cover design for Westinghouse Electric Corporation

Part 2

48' House
© Daniel Hennessy Photography
(pp. 92, 95, 98-100, 104 bottom left and right, 105)
© Chad Loucks (p. 104 top)

E-X-I-T
© Chad Loucks (p. 129)
© IA (pp. 118, 121-123, 125-127)

Tending,(blue)
© Timothy Hursley (pp. 134-135, 137, 140-141, 144 right, 145)
© IA (p. 144 top left and bottom left)

Notes No. 2

2.02 From pinkcomma gallery, Boston, MA

2.04 Georgina Gustin, "The New American Home: Houston, TX," *Dwell*, October 2007

2.08 "Klip House," in *16 Houses: Designing the Public's Private House*, ed. Michael Bell (New York: Monacelli Press, 2004)

2.09 Photographer unknown

2.10 Tupperware order form, Brownie Wise Papers, Archives Center, National Museum of American History, Smithsonian Institution

2.11 Lustron House, Columbus, OH, April 16, 1949. Photo by Arnold Newman Properties/Getty Images

2.12 Sheila Dewan, "Home Despots," *Houston Press*, November 19, 1998

2.13 *I.D. Magazine*, July 1999

2.13 "Klip House," in *Droog Design in Context: Less + More*, ed. Renny Ramakers (Rotterdam: 010 Publishers, 2002). Cover design: thonik.nl

2.13 Eileen Daspin, "Just One Word: Plastics," *Wall Street Journal*, January 22, 1999, W1, W10

2.15 Dawn Finley, "Assuming Risk," *Log*, no. 5 (Spring/Summer 2005): 37-39

2.16 © Chad Loucks

2.18 Michael Bell and Sze Tsung Leong, *Slow Space* (New York: Monacelli Press, 1998). Cover design: Rebecca Mendez

System of Novelties

2.19   Photographer unknown

2.20   Astrodome groundbreaking ceremony,
        1962. Credit: Dan Hardy HP/© Houston
        Chronicle. Used with permission

2.21   Inventor: Mark Scott Wamble

2.22   *ARCHITECT Magazine*, July 2016.
        Photographer Peter Molick

2.23   UL and the UL logo are trademarks of
        UL, LLC

2.25   © Eugene Cook
        Marion Muller and Dick Hess,
        *Dorfsman & CBS: A 40-Year Commitment
        to Excellence in Advertising and
        Design* (New York: American Showcase,
        1987), 38-39

2.27   Digital Image © The Museum of
        Modern Art/Licensed by SCALA / Art
        Resource, NY

2.28   Blaine Brownell, ed., *Transmaterial*
        (Princeton, NJ: Princeton
        Architectural Press, 2006), 205

2.29   © Timothy Hursley

2.30   William Dudley Hunt Jr., *Total
        Design: Architecture of Welton
        Becket and Associates* (New York:
        McGraw-Hill, 1972), 40, 43

2.34   © Hester+Hardaway

Part 3

Yoga Studio and Garden
© Jack Mussett (pp. 174-175, 186, 189)
© Benjamin Hill Photography (p. 180 bottom)
© Hester+Hardaway (p. 170)
© IA (pp. 180 top, 181, 187, 190-191)

Inside Corner
© Jack Mussett and Susan George
(pp. 238, 240-243, 250-253)

Notes No. 3

3.06   © Hester+Hardaway

3.07   *Architecture*, July 2002
        Design architect Mark Wamble with
        the office Bricker+Cannady

3.10   Houston, Texas. August 29, 2017.
        Marcus Yam, *Los Angeles Times*, via
        Getty Images

3.11   Channel steel, royalty-free photo

3.12   Photographer unknown

3.15   © Risa Boyer Leritz. Supergraphic
        by Barbara Stauffacher Solomon, Sea
        Ranch, CA

3.15   Graphic design by William Grover,
        1968. Photo by Yale Joel/The LIFE
        Picture Collection via Getty Images

3.16   Zhenqin Dong and Claire Chalifour

3.19   Artist Norman Wilkinson,
        Encyclopædia Britannica, vol. 30
        (1922)

3.20   © Chad Loucks

3.21   "The Quest for Color," *National
        Geographic*, July 1999, 82-83

3.26   © Jack Mussett and Susan George

3.27   © Jack Mussett and Susan George

Despite extensive research efforts, we
were not able to identify the holders of
all copyright and printing rights for the
images presented. Copyright holders not
identified are asked to contact the author
to claim standard practice remuneration.

Interloop—Architecture

Published with support from:
Rice School of Architecture and Rice
University Creative Ventures Fund

© 2022 Dawn Finley and Park Books AG,
Zurich
© for the texts: Dawn Finley

Published by:
Park Books AG
Niederdorfstrasse 54
8001 Zurich
Switzerland
www.park-books.com

Park Books is being supported by the
Federal Office of Culture with a general
subsidy for the years 2021-2024.

All rights reserved. No part of this
work may be reproduced or edited
using electronic systems, copied, or
distributed in any form whatsoever
without previous written consent from
the publisher.

ISBN 978-3-03860-245-3

Architecture at Rice is the publication
platform of the Rice School of
Architecture in Houston, Texas, an
essential medium for sharing projects
and ideas developed at the school
with audiences worldwide. These publi-
cations synthesize a broad spectrum
of architectural research into a curated
conversation on the current state of
the discipline and its engagement with
the world.

Architecture at Rice
Rice University School of Architecture
MS-50
6100 Main Street
Houston, Texas 77005
www.arch.rice.edu

Title:
System of Novelties

Subtitle:
Dawn Finley and
Mark Wamble,
Interloop—Architecture

Author:
Dawn Finley,
Houston, Texas

Graphic Design:
NORMAL,
Chicago, Illinois

Editor:
Christopher Davey,
Bolton, Connecticut

Research Assistants:
Yumeng An, Adam Berman,
and Yun Koo,
Houston, Texas

Proofreader:
Dean Drake,
Leeds, United Kingdom

Image editing,
printing, and binding:
DZA Druckerei zu
Altenburg GmbH, Thuringia